D0921564

"I thought I already knew how to cope with stress on the job. Then I read Ann Utterback's *Broadcaster's Survival Guide*. I found out that my methods were really destructive, not helpful. I've put some of her tips to work, and Ann's practical advice has really helped me become a better broadcaster."
Dan Shelley, News Director, WTMJ Radio, Milwaukee, Wisconsin

"Ann Utterback knows broadcasters and the stresses we work under. She has managed to package everything that broadcasters need to improve their lives and performances in this one book. No one could ask for a better tool."
Jeff Alan, News Director, WPTY-TV, Memphis, Tennessee

"News folks are real people, too. At least we'd like to think so. Ann Utterback reminds us of this with her *Broadcaster's Survival Guide*. If you're too stressed to read it, have someone who loves you read it to you! You'll both be glad you did."
Lucy Himstedt Riley, News Director, WSFA-TV, Montgomery, Alabama
Chairwoman-Elect, Radio-Television News Directors Association

"No one knows how to calm a stressed-out news director better than Ann Utterback. Her survival guide is right on target."
Janet Evans, News Director, KLBJ radio, Austin, Texas

"Dr. Utterback's book is a must read for anyone in this business, both in front of the camera and behind the scenes. She really understands the toll a career in news can extract from a person, and her book offers ways to cope with the pressures and stresses to prevent burn-out! *Broadcaster's Survival Guide* is mandatory reading if you want to survive and succeed!"
Page Hopkins, Anchor, News 12 New Jersey

"Discovering other interests has not only made me a happier person but a better sportscaster. Everyone needs a helpful hint to—Get a life! This book serves as the perfect reminder."
Chris McKendry, Anchor/reporter, SportsCenter, ESPN

"Stress kills—especially careers in broadcasting. That's why everyone in the business should read this book. Whether you're a veteran anchor or a budding producer, Ann Utterback's simple techniques will help you achieve the success you've always dreamed of."
Cassie Seifert, Co-anchor, PBS, Nightly Business Report

Broadcaster's Survival Guide

Staying Alive in the Business

Ann S. Utterback, Ph.D.

Bonus Books, Inc., Chicago

This book has been researched and written with the best medical and scientific information and assistance available to the author. This book offers recommendations only, however, and not substitutions for conventional medical guidance. Always consult a physician when making any changes in your diet, exercise, or treatment of illness. All matters regarding your health require medical supervision. This book is sold with the understanding that the author is not engaged in rendering psychological, medical, or health services. If expert assistance or counseling is needed, the reader should seek assistance from a professional in the appropriate field. No responsibility will be taken by the author.

The Holmes-Rahe Social Readjustment Ratings Scale in Chapter 3 is reprinted with permission from *Journal of Psychosomatic Research* 11(2), 1967: 213-218, Elsevier Science Inc.

01 00 99 98 97   5 4 3 2 1

Utterback, Ann S.
    Broadcaster's survival guide : staying alive in the business / Ann
S. Utterback.
        p.   cm.
    Includes bibliographical references and index.
    ISBN 1-56625-092-7
    1. Broadcast journalists—Psychological aspects.   2. Stress management.
I. Title.
PN4784.B75U88   1997
070.1´9´019—dc21   97-15717
                                                              CIP

Bonus Books, Inc.
160 East Illinois Street
Chicago, Illinois 60611

Printed in the United States of America

Contents

Survival Technique #4: Learn More About It

Acknowledgments

There have been many people who have contributed to this book by sharing their wisdom. I am indebted to them all.

One wise person once said to me, "Ann, having control in life is important, but learning to let go of control is important as well." This advice helped me learn to let go of some of my behaviors that were increasing my stress. This has allowed me to care for and honor myself. He also pointed out that my work and my life are not separate parts of who I am, and balance is important. I will always be grateful to him for that and for his love and support.

I am also grateful to Margrett who has given me love and support and has helped me learn to care for all parts of myself. She has taught me ways to deal with stress that have changed my life.

A special thanks goes to the broadcast journalists who have provided information for the facing pages you see in some chapters. They are friends and clients who have taught me, as all my clients have, about the pressures of working in broadcasting.

I am not an expert on all the subjects covered in this book. No one could be. For that reason, I have drawn extensively from reference materials which you will see in the endnotes and Suggested Reading sections.

In addition to the use of printed sources, I also called on the expertise of specialists to review material in the book when appropriate. I would like to thank the following professionals for their careful reading of the parts of the text that were within their specialized areas:

Deborah Goldberg, M.D., Board Certified Physician in Internal Medicine and Geriatrics, Cameron Medical Group, Silver Spring, MD. (3. Coping With Stress)

Carolyn E. Crump, Ph.D., Research Coordinator, The University of North Carolina Center for Health Promotion and Disease Prevention, Chapel Hill, N.C. (4. Getting The Exercise You Need)

Margie Ginsberg, M.P.H., R.D., Licensed Nutritionist, Silver Spring, MD (5. Getting The Nutrition You Need)

Karan S. Kverno, Ph.D., R.N., C.S., Director of Biofeed-back and Behavioral Therapies, Medical Illness Counseling Center, Chevy Chase, MD (6. Learning To Relax)

Gwen L. Olive, M.S.W., L.C.S.W.-C., psychotherapist specializing in anxiety disorders, Silver Spring, MD (6. Learning to Relax)

Michael H. Arenstein, M.D., Otolaryngologist, Gaithers-burg, MD (7. Avoiding Pitfalls: Common Cold section)

David P. Feron, P.E., Feron Engineering Associates, Derwood, MD (7. Avoiding Pitfalls: Sick Building Syndrome)

Thanks to Faith Duvall-Menestrina for helping me organize my life so that there was room in it to write this book. I appreciate her assistance and friendship.

And I am grateful to my brother, Jim Smith, who is the only person I know who could find a quote in "Paradise Lost" for me in a matter of minutes. His intelligence has always inspired and amazed me.

I am especially indebted to Dan Shelley, News Director, WTMJ Radio, for reading the entire manuscript and giving me suggestions that improved this book. As a working journalist, he had insights that I didn't, and they were always accurate. I appreciate his respect for my deadlines, his thoroughness, and his humor.

And finally, as always, I want to thank my husband, Jim, who for over thirty years has given me a solid foundation in my life while encouraging me to soar.

Thank you all.

Ann S. Utterback
Washington, D.C.

Foreword

The camera never lies. Over time, the true nature of any broadcaster becomes clear to viewers. Indeed, study after study shows that viewers both respect people who are well-rounded and trust people with whom they can identify. Those are among the many reasons why it is important for broadcast journalists to find balance in their lives.

Unfortunately, the same drive and single-minded focus on work that helps many broadcast journalists land jobs in a highly competitive field are not always the same qualities that help them succeed in those positions over the long term. A life that is devoted primarily to work and career development is not a complete life. It does not result in the evolution of a whole human being. The missing elements show on the air and in the voice in many subtle ways.

Much of the best journalism develops out of personal experience. But people who work almost all of the time and think about work the rest of the time, as many broadcast journalists do, eventually find that they don't have room left in their lives for much personal development. And then they often find that their careers falter.

It's an easy trap to be lured into. The industry is highly competitive, the work is addictively stimulating, and the public recognition gives most of us access and authority well beyond our years and experience. But a heavy volume of high quality work cannot be produced year after year without caring for the mind, the body and the soul. Not all of those things can be accomplished at work.

Ann Utterback reminded me of these things nearly two years ago when I was considering leaving the business. I had achieved my goal of becoming a network anchor, but I was feeling unfulfilled. Our time together convinced me to carry on — but in a different way. I have learned to set limits and to recognize that sometimes taking time out for myself is the best thing I can do to improve my work. Since then, I have produced stories and programs that have helped to improve the lives of thousands of viewers, that have won major journalism awards, and that have brought me both notoriety and financial reward.

I have been able to do so because I learned to accept that sometimes the best thing I can do for my program is not to generate an extra story every single day but to make time for myself every day. That's not always easy to do in an industry where aggressiveness and tenacity are highly valued. The fact is, however, it works.

I first came to Ann for coaching nearly ten years ago when I was working on my vocal technique and trying to make the transition from field producer to on-air reporter. I worked with Ann again when I moved into the anchor chair a few years later. I have kept in touch with her ever since for regular "tune-ups," and I have referred many of my colleagues to her. She remains a trusted friend and confidant. That's because she understands something I was told when I was just out of college and working for CBS News — to remember that "it's only television." Broadcast journalism is important work, but it can neither be done well nor accepted by viewers if it is not generated by people with balance in their lives.

It's a great pleasure to be asked to write the foreword for this book. It should probably be subtitled, "Zen and the Art of Broadcasting." If you adopt even a few of Ann's suggestions, both your work and your life will improve. I've seen it happen for my colleagues, and it has happened for me. For six years now, I have co-anchored the most-watched business news program on television. We have more than twice as many viewers as our closest competitor, and our ratings keep climbing as new competition develops. But more importantly, we do stories that make a difference in our viewers' lives. We are able to do that because we have lives of our own. Much of the credit goes to Ann Utterback.

Cassie Seifert
Co-anchor
Public Television's *Nightly Business Report*

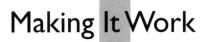

1

Making It Work

Making It Work

*God has given us a world that nothing but our own folly
keeps from being a paradise.*
George Bernard Shaw

You would not have picked up this book unless you felt
that something was not working for you in your life
right now. Because you are reading this, you have a certain
degree of motivation to make a change, but your first question may be, "how do I make this change?" Many times we
think our lives are set on a course that's unalterable like a
run-away train. As out of control as that may feel, making
changes may feel even more unmanageable.

While I was writing this book, I had the pleasure of
being one of four panelists for a roundtable discussion at the
Radio-Television News Directors Association Conference in
Los Angeles. This roundtable was entitled, "Managing
Stress Before It Manages You." The overall feeling I got from
the seventy or so broadcasters who attended was that all this
stuff about stress control sounds good, but it won't work in
real life. I could sense that a lot of people were filtering every
idea that was presented through their own pessimism. They
were thinking that you can't put stress control and their

newsroom in the same sentence because the two can never coexist.

This experience made me even more committed to getting this book in the hands of people like you. I've always believed that knowledge can change things, and I firmly believe that knowledge about stress and its effects can motivate people to make changes. This book is based on that premise.

What this book gives you are Survival Techniques to help you face the stress in your life and deal with it in a healthy way. These are like tools that you might buy in a hardware store. I often tell clients that all I can do is give them tools, and what they build with the tools is their work. Some people may decide to leave the tools where they found them and go on with their lives as before. Others, and I hope you, will take one or two of them (or perhaps all of them) and build a life that works in the best possible way for themselves.

Sometimes it's also important to take the tools and store them away for the future. Change of any kind is always scary. Only you know if this is the right time for you to pursue a change. It's very important that you honor your own time schedule. A change like quitting smoking, for example, will only happen when you are really ready and committed to having it happen. So it may be that you read some of this book and put it away for a period of time until you feel ready to start. There's no timetable except your own. With anything you find in this book, I invite you to use your own guidance as to whether it is correct for you. My goal has been to work like a research assistant for you by collecting information. What you do with this information is entirely up to you.

If you decide to make some lifestyle changes, what benefits can you expect? First of all, I've witnessed during more than a decade of working with broadcasters that there are two ways to sabotage a career. One is to do lousy work, which has not been the case of any client I have worked with or of any broadcaster I have met. The other is to become too stressed about your work so that you can't perform to the best of your ability. As a broadcast voice specialist, I can tell you without any hesitation that stress is the biggest enemy of good delivery. A tense body will always produce a tense voice. If you're an on-air broadcaster, one benefit of learning to deal with stress in a healthy way is that your presentation will improve.

What if you're not on-air? You will find that you are more focused when you work. You will cope better with day-to-day stresses and feel less anxiety. Your energy level will improve in everything you do. You will gain a perspective on your life that you might not have had before. You may begin to feel, as author Stephen Levine describes, that "life is not an emergency."[1]

In addition to these benefits, scientific studies are proving that you will also be healthier. The connection between our immune system and stress is becoming scientific fact, not fiction. We know now that our emotional well-being and our physical well-being are linked.

I have seen this connection over and over in clients with whom I have worked. These clients and every broadcaster I have met over the years have been my teachers. They have shown me what needs to be addressed in a book like this. You will find many examples taken from my encounters as you read. To honor the confidentiality of my clients, any details that might identify particular people have been changed and many times I have combined events into a single example. But what you read are real events and situations common to working journalists.

I have been very open to learning from broadcasters because I have not been in their shoes. I am not a broadcaster and have never been one. My background is in speech communication. I haven't lived day after day in a newsroom and faced the deadlines and pressures that that entails. But I can tell you that I feel a certain connection because you don't have to be a broadcaster to be stressed.

I have always been driven in my own work. I have written six books, three plays, a novel, and numerous magazine articles. I have three degrees, and I own my own business where I work not just with broadcasters but with Fortune 500 companies and political figures. My overachieving nature began when I was very young and has fueled much of my professional life. But in doing that, it prevented me from having a healthy, balanced life. So in many ways, writing this book was for my personal growth as much as for yours.

I feel that I've been preparing my whole life to write a book about stress. Two specific events in 1970 were the inception of this book. That year I was asked to teach voice and diction while working on my master's degree in speech communication. Because of my stressful life, that same year I also enrolled in my first yoga class at the local YMCA to help me relax. As a voice teacher I discovered my interest in working with people on voice improvement, and the yoga class helped me begin to search for some balance in my life.

Now, more than twenty-five years later, I am still on that path. The survival techniques described in this book are a culmination of what works for me on a daily basis. They help me balance my overachieving tendencies with stress-relieving techniques that make my life work in a healthier way. I don't always achieve a perfect balance. In fact, many days stress is the winner. But if I slip one day, I simply get back on track the next day. Socrates said, when asked how to get to Mt. Olympus, to just make every step you take, go in that direction. If our intention is to achieve balance, we are always moving in the right direction.

In this book you'll find information about the three basic approaches I take to cope with stress: exercise, nutrition, and relaxation. In addition, you'll learn about the effects of stress on the body. You will also find out about how to deal with special challenges like working when you have a cold, working in an unhealthy environment, working odd hours, and traveling. All of this information is researched and written with the best medical and scientific information I could obtain. Also, each chapter has been reviewed by an expert in the appropriate field (see Acknowledgments). However, you should always consult your physician when making any changes in diet, exercise, or lifestyle. This book is a supplement, not an alternative, to your regular medical care.

Seeking a healthier lifestyle and one that allows you to excel as a broadcaster is one of the best things you can do for yourself. The Chinese definition of "health" is "balance." Finding the right balance in life and work is a goal that can change your life. It can lead you back to a life you may have forgotten. As Stephen Levine points out, ". . . our natural state of being is like the sun which is always shining, always present, though often obscured."[2] It is blocked by the stress in our lives, but those clouds can move away. We can find ways to be productive without being self-destructive. We can have a life that works.

Seeking Balance

From the Newsroom:

Carole Kneeland, News Director
KVUE-24 Television, Austin, Texas

People's lives are frayed by the stress of this business. Sometimes I feel like I'm standing in my office with a baseball bat, and balls are being thrown at me from every direction. I just have to keep on batting. It feels like my life depends on continuing to hit the balls out of the office. I knew this was going to be a stressful job, but I had no idea it would be as stressful as it is. I battled breast cancer my first year as a news director, and this brush with death left me with a real sense that my time here is short, and my desire to accomplish some things besides work has a greater sense of urgency. My mission here on earth is to be a good journalist, but I also realize that I have a mission of being a friend, a wife, a stepmother, and a daughter to people who I really care about. I make sure I give that side of my life the time it needs. My husband and I do a lot of social activities like dinners with friends. We go to a church and are active in a Sunday school where we do things like feed the homeless once a month. I am also in a book club, and I read at least one novel a month. I never used to read a book unless I was on vacation. One wonderful thing I do for myself is that once a week I leave work early and get a full body massage. Besides the relaxation of it, it gets me home by 7 p.m. which means I have an evening when I can do something with my husband. Every day I either ride my indoor bike while I watch the morning news or I walk at night with my husband. I also believe in taking long vacations of at least two weeks. I hear of people who don't take all their vacation days. That's nuts. We also have stress relievers in the newsroom like keeping a sense of humor and giving parties for people. We look for opportunities to get people off to retreats and seminars to give them a one-day break. I used to work every Saturday in the newsroom, and I'd work at home on Sundays. I now always take my weekends. A lot of us are really control freaks, and it helps to just give that up and realize that it's the big things that are important and not the small things. I ignore a lot of small stresses since I had a life-threatening disease. Living is much more important than returning all the phone calls you got that day. When you realize how numbered your days are, it allows you to blow off some things that you might not otherwise. Every friend and family member you have is important, and they deserve to be nurtured. They're going to be there long after this job is over.

·2·

Seeking Balance

*Through Fate there's a balance that's coming.
It's coming for you,
and it's coming for me, too.*
Ferron[1]

Finding balance in your life when you work in broadcasting is not easy. One television anchor outlined the challenge for me. She works at the station ten to twelve hours a day. In her off-hours she runs to the dry cleaner's and the grocery and does all the things that are necessary to keep her life going. She also spends many hours participating in events for local charities for the station. Her schedule leaves her no time to rest and relax. Her complaint was that she wakes up all through the night with a "To Do" list in her head. She can't get back to sleep easily which leaves her exhausted. Her anchoring suffers because she has low vocal energy at the anchor desk and difficulty focusing on her news copy. In addition, she is sick more often and stays ill longer because of her exhaustion. She knows she can't continue at this pace without getting complaints about her on-air performance and possibly becoming very ill. She is finding that she can't separate her lifestyle from her performance style. She feels like she's going a hundred miles an hour toward a brick wall, and her fear is that unless she makes some lifestyle changes she will hit that wall.

This anchor is not unique in the difficulties she faces daily. Balancing work and other activities is challenging for most people, but for broadcasters it's especially difficult (see Figure 2.1). Broadcasting is a very stressful profession with constant deadlines and crises. As you'll see in the next chapter, stress is a factor that affects broadcasters on many levels. In fact, no other profession is more stressful than being on live television or radio. Even brain surgeons and air traffic controllers can have someone take over for them and have a break. But if you're on live television or radio, there's no walking off the set. You have to be able to perform well under intense pressure. The same is true for news directors, producers, writers, and others who work in the industry. When a deadline is looming, everyone has to be able to function at peak level under intense pressure. One news director told me she often feels like she's in the famous "I Love Lucy" candy factory skit. One crisis follows another, and it's a challenge to keep up.

Most broadcasters can cope with the usual stresses like deadlines, computers or TelePrompTers malfunctioning, and late-breaking news. They are skilled at working under pressure. What creates difficulty are the life pressures that impinge on that. You may feel that if you had someone to take care of all the other pressures in your life like relationship and family issues, housecleaning, cooking, buying groceries, etc., you would have no problems. But that's not an option for many of us. Consequently, what happens is that other stressors become layered on top of the chronic stress of the business. It may not be difficult to manage the daily stress of working in a newsroom and going on air. That's part of a normal day. But layer a simple task like getting a car repaired or seeing a child's teacher into that day, and it

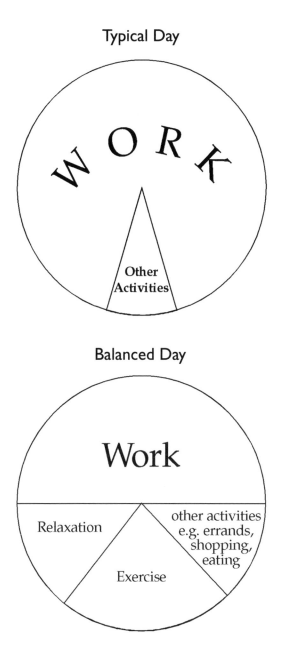

Figure 2.1 Each day should be balanced to include activities outside of our work life.

becomes overwhelming because it is layered on top of so many other stressors.

Stress also comes from increased pressures at work. Consider the demands of covering a severe crisis like a major snow storm, airplane crash, or other disaster that requires working days without much rest. There may also be times when staff cut-backs or a station buy-out happen. These extraordinary work situations add additional layers of stress.

And when stress builds up, it affects the body in significant ways. The results of being overwhelmed can be as severe as having a panic attack at the anchor desk.

One anchor had worked with me for months because she was experiencing panic attacks, and she wanted to improve her breathing which is what she thought was the problem. When she lost her breathing rhythm she would get hot all over and feel as if she was going to faint. She had experienced many of the symptoms of panic attacks which are explained in Chapter 3. I had helped her with breathing and suggested ways of coping with the attacks, but they persisted. It was not until she happened to mention to me one day that her divorce would be final that week that it all made sense. When I asked when her panic attacks began she told me they started about the time she and her husband separated. This is an example of layering a very stressful event like a divorce onto what was already a stressed life. This additional layer of stress had been more than she could handle and had pushed her into having panic attacks. Had I known about the divorce, I would have suggested that she seek counseling to work with her feelings during the separation and divorce. This would have made it more likely that she could get through this difficult time without her on-air performance suffering.

Effects of Stress

There are two ways that excessive stress affects broadcasters. First, it impedes good on-air performance. Secondly, it increases the likelihood that a broadcaster will become ill and stay ill longer.

On-Air Delivery

How does stress affect on-air delivery? It's obvious that stress affects our ability to think clearly, but it affects our bodies as well. When we speak, the voice is produced within the larynx by folds of tissue in the throat. These folds of tissue include muscle. In fact, muscles play a critical role in vocal production. The tongue which we use to articulate words is a very large muscle. Our jaw is controlled by muscles. The diaphragm which contributes to breathing is a large floor of muscle that separates our abdominal cavity from our thoracic cavity. Muscles respond to tension, and that tension can come from other parts of the body. One muscle can respond to tension elsewhere. In many ways, our entire body is our instrument of speech. Any physical limitations we have may create vocal limitations.

The best on-air performance style is one that is relaxed and natural. We no longer want "announcers" in broadcasting. What we want are comfortable communicators. The highest rated anchors are the ones who give the impression that they can sit at the anchor desk and cover an event for as long as needed. And while they do this, they remain calm even in the most severe crisis. I call this the "Eight-hour Test." Would you want to watch or listen to this person for eight hours, and could they maintain good vocal energy? With good vocal energy they stay focused on their material and their listeners without appearing to be "on" all the time. Some anchors give the impression that they will be lucky to make it through a thirty-minute broadcast because they are trying so hard to appear energetic. A comfortable delivery doesn't look like a performance.

Audiences are very skilled at reading subtle aspects of a person's delivery. Think of the last time you called a friend who was stressed. Didn't you hear that in the person's voice? The same is true when a friend has had a bad day and is sad or depressed. We hear it immediately. We know if a person is bored or stressed or tired just by the sound of their voice. No matter how hard a professional broadcaster may try to conceal these things, they often come through to the audience. It's difficult to stay focused on ideas when stress builds up. Stress causes on-air broadcasters to stumble more on words and to have difficulty with breathing and pausing. These are all signals to the listener that this person is stressed. The good news is that they can be signals to us as well to help us control our stress levels before they affect on-air delivery.

Others in the newsroom project stress with their voices as well. If you're a news director, producer, camera person or anyone else in a newsroom, you have a responsibility to deal with your stress. When a crisis occurs, no one in the newsroom should increase the urgency of the crisis by screaming or losing control. The ambience of the newsroom is affected by the way all the staff communicates.

The chronic stress of working in broadcasting is never going to change. The very definition of working in the news business means that you will have to deal with stress every day. And there are always stressors in daily life as well. Unless you can afford to have every detail of your life outside of work handled by someone else, chances are you are going to face daily life stresses. These will range from simple things like car trouble to difficult challenges like divorce, deaths of loved ones, and illness. You truly can't wall off your life from your work in terms of stress. They are interrelated whether you like it or not.

And you can't wall off the effects of stress on your body. The effects of stress are in the mind and in the body as well. For on-air broadcasters, your bodies are your vocal instruments, and your bodies exist in the contexts of your lives. As the stress of your lives plays itself out in your bodies, it plays itself out in on-air performance as well.

Health

But stress doesn't just affect the voice. The second way that stress is harmful to broadcasters may be even more important than the first because stress affects the body's natural ability to defend itself against illness. One study showed that injecting a small amount of adrenaline into a patient caused an immediate decline in helper cells (lymphocytes) in the body.[2] Adrenaline is one of the hormones that our bodies produce when we are stressed. Helper cells augment the immune response which allows us to fight off illness. Even a small amount of excess adrenaline affects the body's ability to stay well. This is why the stress of being a broadcaster may make it harder to fight off colds and viruses and more difficult to get well once an illness has manifested itself.

In Chapter 3 we will see that there is positive stress and negative stress. The interesting thing about negative stress is that it is our inability to feel in control of the stress that makes it harmful. It's the feeling of helplessness that really affects us. In my own life I have seen this in action. If I'm feeling confident and in control, I can be in a room full of people sneezing and coughing with colds and stay perfectly healthy. But if I feel overwhelmed by stress and the thought goes through my head that I wish I could just spend a week in bed, I can get a cold when all those around me are healthy.

The medical profession is realizing that we can't isolate the mind from the body. A new area of medicine called psychoneuroimmunology studies the body's interconnections. The theory of this new area of medicine is best summed up by author Deepak Chopra when he says, "Our immune system eavesdrops on our thoughts." What we think and how we live have a direct influence on our wellness. If you doubt this, look at some of the studies dating back over forty years that show the positive effect of a placebo. A placebo has been proven to have as great as a 37 percent chance of working as well as any medicine.[3] If we believe something in our minds, it appears that our bodies believe it as well.

Most of our medical history in this country has worked on the premise that you can cure a disease in isolation as if it doesn't exist in a thinking person. Rene Descartes, a 17th century philosopher, proposed this idea that the mind is separate from the body. Physicians have viewed the body as working like a machine with mechanical laws for over a hundred years.

Now the medical profession is realizing that unless they include a person's mind, emotions, and lifestyle choices in the recovery process, the disease will return. An example of this is bypass surgery for a blocked coronary artery. If the patient has bypass surgery, but the patient's lifestyle remains the same, the arteries will block again. The approach that works is to follow surgery with lifestyle changes such as increasing aerobic exercise, eating better, relaxing more, and giving up harmful activities like smoking. Combining these with surgery is highly effective.

Physicians began recognizing this back in 1979 when the Surgeon General, Julius B. Richmond, M.D., stated that as many as half of the nation's premature deaths could be due to unhealthy behaviors and lifestyles. Of the top ten leading causes of premature death he reported that at least seven could be reduced by altering bad habits like poor diet, smoking, alcohol abuse, lack of exercise, and unhealthy responses to stress.[4]

Recognizing that the mind and body are connected and operate as a unit has changed Western medicine. Illness is now seen as being influenced by many things such as genetics, nutrition, emotional stress, environmental factors such as toxic exposure, and lack of exercise.

I have watched my approach to work as a broadcast voice specialist follow the same path as the medical profession. When I began I believed that I could focus only on voice problems and see results. It was as if I could take someone's larynx out like a carburetor on a car and fix it and then put it back into their body. I expected things to run smoothly after this procedure. What I found repeatedly, however, was that if that person was overly stressed nothing I did for them would help. I could teach them everything I knew about voice and load them down with vocal exercises, but if stress was a factor the problem they were experiencing would return. What I realized was that stress is like dirty gasoline in a car. If you put a clean carburetor in a car with dirty gasoline, it will malfunction again. All the benefits of your work will be lost, and you'll have to continue to clean the carburetor over and over. When I began to focus on stress and lifestyle issues that might be impeding vocal improvement, I found that the improvement lasted.

Taking Care of Your Body

What I also found is that most people take better care of their cars than they do their bodies. We don't run our cars without gasoline, but many people don't eat and give their bodies the fuel they need. We take our cars in for routine maintenance, but many people don't seek help for chronic headaches, sleep problems, and other physical problems that affect their lives. We hear the first knock in our engine and have it checked out, but we become used to overriding physical cues from our bodies that tell us something is wrong. One extreme example of this came from a client who told me she had actually trained herself not to have to go to the bathroom because she didn't want to be called away from a big news event. This is a potentially life-threatening way to override the body's basic needs.

Unfortunately, broadcasters, like the general population, may also use drugs to turn off the body's physical cues that signal something is wrong. Taking aspirin for a headache is fine, but when you turn to prescription and recreational drugs including alcohol, tranquilizers, sleeping medications, and anxiety reducing drugs, you're masking the symptoms that should tell you something is wrong in your body. I have had more than one client tell me they are taking Xanax (a benzodiazepine) or Inderal (a beta-andrenergic blocking agent) to deal with their anxiety. These drugs may be necessary for short periods of time, but in the long run it works best to deal with the stress that is causing the symptoms instead of treating the symptoms alone.

Listening to cues from your body and taking care of your body is not a luxury when you're in broadcasting. It's a necessity because in broadcasting you will face chronic stress year after year. Making healthy lifestyle changes and sticking with them must happen to have a good, comfortable on-air delivery if you're an anchor or reporter in radio or television. If you're a news director, producer, camera person, or have any other job in a newsroom, you are faced with the same chronic stress. Recognizing the effects of this stress on your body and mind and making lifestyle changes to cope with the stress will help you perform better on the job and stay healthy. And if you're a student who is thinking of going into the field of broadcasting, there is no better time to begin setting good habits that will enhance your career.

Keep in mind that all news operations want you to work as many hours as you can at peak performance. Many news directors and general managers will help you do this in a healthy manner, but some news operations may not always have your best interest in mind. It's important as a professional in the field to set your own boundaries at times to help you take care of yourself. If you're sick with a cold, it's to your advantage to take sick leave. As you'll see in Chapter 7 this can save your voice and get you back to work faster. If you have worked too many hours and are exhausted, it's wise to go home instead of working an extra shift.

Thinking of your needs should begin when you or your agent negotiate your contract. Instead of seeing a higher salary as your only goal, think of other negotiables like more vacation days. Vacation is not something to take lightly as a broadcaster. You need to have as much vacation as you can negotiate in your contract, and you need to *take* that vacation. Studies with heart attack patients have shown that the frequency of patients' vacations is inversely proportional to the number and seriousness of their heart attacks.[5] Get vacation days allotted to you and take the vacation on a regular basis. Even one day off a month will help you cope with stress and stay healthy. It's no badge of honor to brag about all the vacation days you've amassed. It's only a sign that you're not taking care of yourself.

But don't see vacation as the only negotiable item for a contract. There are other requests that can make a big difference for you and that are relatively inexpensive for a station. For example, one television anchor negotiated for a health spa membership so she could work-out easily each day. Another got a membership at an aquatic center close to the newsroom so that he could swim before work for exercise and relaxation. One talent agent told me she always negotiates benefits that will improve the quality of life for her clients and will help relieve stress, like golf and tennis club memberships, first class airline travel, and dry cleaning services for professional clothes. Clothing allowances and make-up artists also make life easier. In larger markets limousine service might even be an option especially when working late hours. You may think that this kind of negotiating is not possible, but there are always changes both big and small that can make your life more manageable.

You may also feel you don't have the time to make even simple healthy changes in your life. But if you've read this far, you're motivated to make a change. The topics covered in the following chapters will give you more information about stress and how to combat it in your life. You'll find easy changes you can pursue in the "Healthy Suggestions" section that follows each chapter. These will make a difference for you every day. You may think you can't afford the time, but how can you *not* afford it if it will improve your quality of life and make you better at your job?

Healthy Suggestions

At the end of each chapter you will find a section like this with some Healthy Suggestions of ways to add some health-enhancing activities to your life. Pick the ones that you like the most and put them on a card or in a notebook so that you can read over them often. Make them part of your life. As with any exercise or activity, do not continue anything that causes you pain either physically or emotionally. Make wise decisions about what works for you.

1 One of the first things that disappears from life when we become stressed is real joy. On a piece of paper, list some activities that you have enjoyed in your life outside of work. These might include hobbies you've done or trips you've taken or any activity that you've really enjoyed. Now opposite each of these things write down the last time you participated in that activity. This may give you an idea of how deprived your life has been of things that make you happy. The absence of good events may be more stressful than the presence of stress itself. Studies have shown that the simple act of petting a dog or cat can lower your blood pressure. So give yourself permission to include some of these activities that you enjoy in your daily life. This is no luxury. It's very necessary to your ability to perform well in broadcasting.

2 On a piece of paper write your wish-list for the perfect contract. If you could negotiate for things that would help you stay healthy and feel less stressed, what would they be? Don't eliminate any possibility. Let this list include your most outrageous ideas as well as fairly realistic ones. Keep this list and refer to it every time you get a new job. Who knows, in a few years requesting to work at home part of each week

or to have a personal trainer come in every day to help you exercise might not be so outrageous.

3 Now that most newsrooms are smoke-free, it's common practice for smokers to go outside two, three, or four times a day or more to smoke. I strongly believe that nonsmokers should get the same rights. Clients often tell me that they have to stay glued to their desks to get all their work done. I point out to them that the person sitting right next to them with the same workload goes out to smoke several times a day. There is no reason you can't take "nonsmoker breaks." Go out of the building. Walk around and look at the scenery and let yourself forget about the pressures of the newsroom. This may take less than five minutes, but you'll come back refreshed and re-laxed without the toxic chemicals in your body that smoking gives you.

4 Imagine you have been diagnosed with a chronic illness like multiple sclerosis or diabetes. Write down all the ways you would change your lifestyle to take better care of yourself. For example, you might concentrate on your diet more or you might begin ex-ercising. If you smoke, you would certainly quit. Why wait until an illness strikes to make these changes? It has been proven that many illnesses can be avoided by making healthy changes in lifestyle. Make them today.

Coping With Stress

From the Newsroom:

Chris Houston, Assignment Editor
WUSA-TV, Washington, D.C.

As an Assignment Editor I may arrive at work thinking that my day isn't going to be that stress-filled, and as soon as I walk in the door, wham, it hits. I see everyone running around on some breaking story, and I have to jump right in the mix. The bad news about this is that my mind has to start going a million miles an hour. I have to try to think of the situation and how we're going to deal with it. I begin to look at my watch, and we're always getting closer and closer to air time. The news director may be breathing down my neck. I may have a reporter who's not putting forth much effort or a photographer who didn't get the right shot. Or maybe my live truck is not where it should be. Sometimes this stress is good, and I get a real adrenaline rush and an energy charge. Other days, it's not so good because maybe I don't feel like working under that pressure. I have to get in gear regardless and do the best I can, but that builds a lot of stress. It's really tough to come home after that. I get off work after the eleven o'clock newscast so at eleven-thirty or midnight I am walking in the door at home supercharged. There are some nights when I don't go to sleep until three or four o'clock in the morning because I have such an adrenaline rush that I have to come down. I also notice that I get more headaches. One of the dangers I have is that on a big story I forget to eat or drink water. Sometimes I even forget to go to the bathroom. I work a whole shift and my body's telling me, wait a minute, you haven't eaten in twelve hours. I know that's not good for my body. And then when I go on vacation, after a few days it's weird, but I miss the stress. Maybe it's an addiction, but it's hard to do anything at normal speed anymore. It's hard to relax. One of the trademarks of a good assignment editor is that even when you're panicked and stressed out you don't show it. You know your reporters and producers are going to be stressed out, but you can't. You are supposed to be the calming influence. You have to keep it all internal and that's hard. And then when you do explode you really explode and that's not good either. I know that normal people don't go through this kind of stress every day in their jobs. Maybe now I'm young enough to handle it, but what happens in ten years? Am I going to end up walking in the door one day and dropping to the floor?

·3·

Coping With Stress

*The brain is capable of holding a conversation with
the body that ends in death.*
Russian Proverb[1]

In Japan, they have a name for it: Karoshi. This means death from overwork. Karoshi claims around 10,000 Japanese annually, some of whom literally drop dead on the job.[2] I often think of this when I talk to over-stressed clients. I wonder if clients would make lifestyle changes if they knew what stress is doing to their bodies. Chronic stress is not just an inconvenience that may give us a headache now and then. It's a life-threatening situation. In this chapter you'll see how the constant release of stress hormones erodes the body on many levels. Stress can sabotage your career and your health. But if you understand how the stress reaction works, you can learn to prevent it and deal with stress in a healthy way.

What Is Stress?

A basic definition of stress doesn't sound too ominous. Basically, stress is "Anything — pleasant or unpleasant — that arouses your adrenaline system and mobilizes your body for flight or fight. . . ."[3] This might be the thrill of riding a roller coaster or the challenge of avoiding another car when your car's in a skid. These events come quickly and leave just as quickly. They produce a healthy stress response (see Figure 3.1). In these events, something triggers a stress reaction, we get a surge of stress hormones to handle the event, and then we rest and relax after the situation has passed. Our bodies have a chance to recover from the stress.

When the definition of stress is expanded, however, to include chronic stress that is unrelenting, the problems with stress emerge. It's the lack of time to recover from the stress response that changes stress from something that is helpful and, at times, life-saving to a destructive and possibly life-threatening disease.

There are times in your life as a broadcaster when you need stress to help you perform better at your job. If you're covering a breaking news event as a reporter, stress is your ally. During a riot or protest demonstration, for example,

Stress Patterns

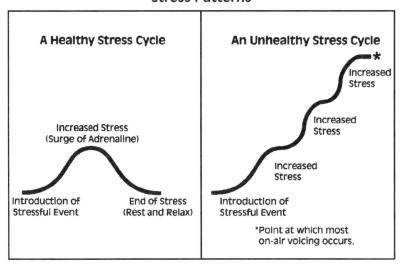

Figure 3.1 Many broadcasters experience unhealthy stress cycles when on air.

you will need the flight or fight response to help you do your job well and avoid getting hurt in the process. If you're a news director, producer, or on the desk, you may need some adrenaline to help you adjust your broadcast to a late-breaking story. But these events should be time-limited. Once the event is over, you should be able to rest and relax.

You may find the idea of resting and relaxing humorous because in most newsrooms one stressful event follows the next. And many times it's not even necessary for another stressful event to pop up to keep us stressed. We often hold onto the stress in our minds, which can be just as powerful as being in the event itself. Our thoughts have the same capability of triggering the stress response as events do. A perceived threat is just as real for us as the actual threat. If the riot has ended, for example, but we continue to think about our coverage of it and how it could have been better, our body is still operating as if it were in the event. The same is true when we lie awake at night reviewing what challenges await us the next day. Our thoughts cause chemical changes in our bodies that communicate with every cell. Stress literally "begins in the *mind* but ends in the *body*."[4] When we think about stressful events, our body pays the price. "It's as if the brain has branch offices in every cell."[5]

If you question that your mind is closely connected with your body, remember the last time you had goose bumps. This reaction is part of the flight or fight response. In animals it causes their fur to bristle which often makes them appear larger and, thus, more formidable opponents. For us, it's a good way to feel the mind affecting the body. Think of a time when you were really cold, actually shivering, or remember when you were suddenly frightened. If you can do this completely enough, your mind will signal your body to respond, and you will get goose bumps. This is one way the mind can signal the body to react.

How Your Body Reacts

The flight or fight response is not something new. It was first written about in the early 1900s by Dr. Walter B. Cannon who was a professor of psychology at Harvard Medical School. He described the ways that the body responds when it is forced to adjust to physical stress like extreme heat, cold, or great exertion, or psychological stress as when the emotions are triggered by a perceived threat.

The body has a complicated and very sophisticated reaction to stress. First, the heart beats faster and harder when it receives a signal from the sympathetic nervous system. This system, also called the autonomic nervous system, deals with bodily responses that are not consciously controlled. The hypothalamus, which is at the base of the brain, signals the adrenal glands above the kidneys to release the more than fifty stress hormones and steroids.[6] The most important of these are adrenaline (also called epinephrine), noradrenaline, and the steroid, cortisol. Adrenaline and noradrenaline are the emergency hormones that help us through a crisis, and cortisol comes into play when we are under chronic stress.

Originally this bodily reaction was life-saving. Humans spent three million years living in forests and deserts and dealing with physical attacks.[7] They dealt with extremes in temperatures and were likely to be fighting for their lives on a daily basis. By contrast, we have only lived around fifty years with modern technology. Our bodies don't realize that what we face now is not life threatening. A computer crashing may seem like the end of the world, but it doesn't compare with the physical challenges our ancestors met. What usually happens now in our lives is that an alarm goes off in our body, but we're not attacked physically. Nonetheless, our body begins the flight or fight response. We get high-level chemicals released in our body for what is really a low-level threat.

Let's look at what the body did for our early ancestors who lived in the wild. If one of our early ancestors were attacked by a bear, he would obviously want to fight or flee. In order to do this, his body would secrete the stress hormones to propel him to action. When danger approached, his bodily systems would react instantly and simultaneously. His metabolism would increase and this would convert food into energy faster. His heart would begin beating faster and harder. At the same time, the blood vessels in his extremities would constrict, allowing more blood to go to his vital organs. This would also reduce bleeding if he were injured. Coupled with this, his blood chemistry would change so that it would clot more easily in case of injury. His breathing would speed up to allow more oxygen for quick thinking and to assist in fighting or fleeing. His digestion would shut down to divert more blood to vital functions. In fact all bodily systems that were not needed for survival would be put on hold. Muscles would contract to create an armor for the body. And his pupils would dilate for better vision. His body would very rapidly become a fighting machine.

Now let's move that reaction into modern time. You're on deadline. You're sitting at your computer and the news story you're writing vanishes from the screen. Your eyes observe this and signal your hypothalamus at the base of your brain to alert your body that something is terribly wrong. The hypothalamus sends the message to the adrenal glands above the kidneys, and they begin secreting adrenaline and the other stress hormones. Before you know it, you're breathing faster and your hands have become icy as you hit every key you can think of to restore your story to the screen. Your blood pressure and heart rate have gone up and the blood vessels to your extremities have constricted. You begin to feel queasy as your digestive system shuts down. Your mouth gets dry as the blood supply to the salivary glands is diverted. All your blood is being channeled to your vital organs so you can fight or flee. These are not appropriate responses to this situation. What is really a small inconvenience has caused your body to go into a major survival mode.

This isolated event in your life might not be destructive to your body. But it's an example of just one of hundreds of stressful events that probably happen to you every day. And for most of us, there's no time to stop and rest and relax after this event occurs. We get the physiological reaction of the flight or fight response, and we continue on with our day facing even more stresses.

In our example, the story is restored to the screen, and we immediately deal with the pressure that comes from the delay the computer glitch caused. The deadline has crept closer which increases stress even more. We have another stress response to deal with. As our day progresses, what should be an emergency response becomes a lifestyle (see Figure 3.1). It's this chronic repetition of the flight or fight response that affects our health.

The Effects of Stress on Your Body

Chronic stress is one of the biggest health problems in this country. It is estimated that stress-related diseases account for seventy-five to ninety percent of visits to primary care physicians. Job stress is considered by many to be the *number one* adult health problem in this country.[8] These statistics are drawn from a cross-section of jobs with varying levels of stress. If you consider the demands of working in broadcasting, the picture looks even grimmer.

Chronic stress erodes almost every part of the body. The most significant damage may be to the heart. Many experts, including Dr. Dean Ornish, a highly respected cardiologist, believe that controlling stress may be the single most important thing you can do to prevent heart disease, the leading killer of Americans.

Every day the heart pumps over 2000 gallons of blood (the equivalent of 100 automobile gasoline tanks) through 60,000 miles of elastic tubing.[9] The flight or fight response causes this tubing, the blood vessels, to constrict and the heart to beat faster and harder. This, coupled with the increased ability of the blood to clot during stress, sets us up for heart problems. And remember that the constriction of the blood vessels can come from emotional stress as well as physical stress. The general manager of your station doesn't have to send that memo reprimanding you, you can simply think about what would happen if he did.

Heart disease studies have also shown that people who are the most prone to have heart problems are ones who are always in a hurry, have a low tolerance for frustration, and are highly driven.[10] That's a perfect description of most people working in broadcasting.

But heart disease is not the only problem that stress creates in the body. Perhaps the most common symptoms are digestive problems. Stress shuts down the digestive system and also creates more acid in the stomach. When stress is chronic, the stomach stays in an upset mode.

In fact, if you're chronically over-stressed you're likely to have one or more of these common symptoms that were described by Drs. Jonathan C. Smith and Jeffrey M. Seidel of Roosevelt University:[11]

Common Symptoms of Stress
1. gastric distress
2. disturbed cardiorespiratory activity
3. restless activity
4. self-consciousness
5. fatigue and lack of energy
6. headaches
7. backaches

8. skin problems
9. shoulder, neck, and back tension
10. trembling or shaking.
   I would add some additional symptoms to this list that I often hear from clients:
11. feeling helpless and/or overwhelmed
12. having emotional outbursts that might include crying or raging
13. feeling the need to be over-controlling
14. having trouble sleeping and/or grinding or clenching teeth
15. drinking alcohol or using other drugs or cigarettes more than usual
16. eating more or less than usual.

Another area where stress affects the body is the immune system. The production of antibodies from amino acids is reduced when we're stressed. Our immune system becomes less hardy. We are more susceptible to viruses and bacteria when we are under stress. We may also sleep poorly or think that we don't need as much sleep. Over time, lack of sleep affects our immune system as well (see Chapter 7).

More of the protein we eat, which should help repair our bodies, is lost when we are stressed. The protein we eat when we're stressed may not be utilized as well as it should be, which can affect our recuperative powers.[12] Research has shown that people under chronic stress heal more slowly than those who are not as stressed.[13]

One reason we lose weight or stay thin when stressed is because of this rerouting of the amino acids. We draw amino acids from our tissues when stressed to use as extra fuel which results in weight loss. We need lots of "flight fuel" when stressed, and our bodies pay the price.[14]

Good Stress Versus Bad Stress

From the sound of things, it would appear that all stress is bad for us. That's not the case. If we eliminated all stress from life, we'd be pretty bored. The occasional crunch of getting a story written at the last minute or the thrill of arranging a great interview, make working in broadcasting exciting. Stress often stimulates us to meet challenges and excel. Remember that a definition of stress is, "Anything — pleasant or unpleasant — that arouses your adrenaline system and mobilizes your body for flight or fight. . . ." The goal is not to get rid of all the stress in life, but to learn how to use the extra stress hormones when you need them. We also must learn when we *really need* them. We shouldn't use this heavy duty response for the sometimes continuous minor irritations in life.

The addictive quality of stress arises, however, because getting a shot of stress hormones in our bodies is rarely an unpleasant feeling. Quite the opposite is true. Noradrenaline actually invigorates us much like a couple of cups of strong coffee with caffeine. We feel energized and confident. We feel we need less sleep, and there's a feeling of excitement. Our performance and efficiency actually improve for a short period of time. We may become convinced that this is the best way to operate for our peak performance.

And when we relax we may feel bad at first. Without the extra stress hormones in our systems we may feel depressed and experience the pain that the stress hormones were masking. Have you ever gotten a bad headache after things calm down in the newsroom? While we're getting the stress hormones we have a false sense of well-being. We may become convinced that the adrenaline and noradrenaline are helping us. But as we've seen, if this release of stress hormones continues over a longer time, the stress response erodes the body in numerous ways.

Dr. Hans Selye, a noted Canadian endocrinologist and the father of stress research, originated the terms "eustress" for good stress and "distress" for bad stress. Both of these move the body away from its normal state and cause stress hormones to be released in the body. But eustress helps us perform better and contributes to our enjoyment of life. Most sports would fall into the eustress category. We may love a heated game of tennis or a vigorous workout on a treadmill. But when these activities end we relax and forget about them (see Figure 3.1). Distress comes when we hold onto the stress and fail to rest and relax. It also comes from the chronic stresses that occur in most newsrooms.

Our bodies have a wonderful skill of adapting to demands placed on them. If you do aerobic exercise, your body will become a better oxygen-using machine (see Chapter 4). Likewise, if you live and work in a stressful environment, the body and mind will adapt. One way that we adapt to stress is by becoming a Type A personality. Dr. Meyer Friedman, who first described Type A behavior, explains it as ". . . a continuous struggle, an unremitting attempt to accomplish or achieve more and more things or participate in more and more events in less and less time, frequently in the face of opposition — real or imagined — from other persons."[15] Type A

Type A Tendencies

1. Tendency to over-plan
2. Multiple thoughts and actions
3. Needs to win
4. Desires recognition
5. Always feels guilty
6. Impatient with delays and interruptions
7. Overextends oneself
8. Sense of time urgency
9. Excessive competitive drive
10. Workaholic.

personalities exhibit three main characteristics: 1) they think continuously, 2) they think and do things rapidly, and 3) they think and do things polyphasically (more than one thing at a time like watching the news, eating, and listening to telephone messages).[16] If those characteristics seem to fit you, see if you can relate to some listed on the previous page.[17]

If you find that more than a few of these relate to you, you might be addicted to stress. Your personality may have become one that has adapted to the demands of stress so much that it's an integral part of your life. If this is true, you have set yourself up for the health problems you read about earlier.

Panic Attacks

One result of too much stress that can have a significant effect on your career is a panic attack. Panic attacks are the best kept secret in the broadcasting profession. Many broadcasters have them, and they often never tell anyone else about them. I have had a large number of clients who have revealed to me that they have suffered from panic attacks or are still plagued by them. And I have seen some careers that have ended because of panic attacks that remained untreated.

A panic attack is the fastest and most complex reaction the human body can experience, and it's not uncommon. As many as three million Americans suffer from panic attacks with women being twice as likely to be affected as men.[18]

What happens when you have a panic attack? Most people say it feels like they are dying. Many people rush to the emergency room convinced that they are having a heart attack or stroke. The reason for this reaction is that a panic attack is like pulling the emergency brake on your car at eighty miles per hour. It's immediate, overpowering, and uncontrollable once it begins. It's the core meltdown of stress. All of the symptoms of stress happen almost instantly in a panic attack.

For many people it begins with difficulty breathing. It may feel like you can't take a deep breath or your breathing may accelerate. This may be accompanied by a tightness in your chest. You might feel a tingling in your hands and feet which quickly moves up the body. You may begin sweating profusely or you may get a cold, clammy feeling. You might become dizzy or you may begin to black out. Your heart races, and you feel nauseated. You may hear your heart pounding. Many of these symptoms are the same as those of a heart attack so it is important to take them seriously.

I have had clients tell me when they experience panic attacks they want to run and hide. Many say they feel trapped. This can happen when you're sitting at the anchor desk. One anchor became so panicked that she actually did run from the anchor desk at a commercial break and was not able to return. Panic attacks often occur during live work in the field. One reporter could not remember where she was in her live shot and froze. Panic attacks can happen in the newsroom as well. The pressure of working any job in a newsroom can be overwhelming. Some people say they begin crying or can't control the urge to laugh even if they are on air. Many say that they feel unreal or cut off from their surroundings (depersonalization). Another common symptom for anchors is that they cannot read the TelePrompTer. The words become blurry or they jump around.

Triggers for panic attacks can come in many forms. They may result from an external event or a change in perception. One client said his mouth would become so dry that he could not articulate his words. Another said that her breathing would get so difficult she would have to stop in the middle of a word to breathe. Weatherman Willard Scott is quoted by the Anxiety Disorder Association of America as saying that his panic attack "really hit me one morning just out of the blue . . . I was on the air one morning and like that, I started to hyperventilate . . . to the point I could barely speak."[19] I had a client who was a radio anchor and experienced a panic attack for the first time when she read a story of childhood abuse on the air that triggered some emotions in her. A television reporter told me he began stumbling when he said the call letters of his station, and the fear of that happening again triggered a panic attack.

When any of these symptoms occur, they create a vicious cycle that escalates the fear. If an anchor has trouble saying a word, fear sets in that it will happen again. This makes it more likely that it will, indeed, happen again. When it happens again, the fear escalates. The cycle can continue until a full-fledged panic attack is triggered. Once this happens another vicious cycle begins which is the fear that the panic attack is not an isolated event. Every on-air appearance is met with increasing fear that another panic attack will occur.

One-time events can trigger panic attacks, but they are usually the result of a build up of stress. All the clients who have confided in me that they are having panic attacks (or have had them in the past), are suffering from several layers of stress. As mentioned in Chapter 2, it's the layers of stress that usually push us over the edge. One television anchor, for example, called me in tears because she suddenly could not breathe on the set. When I asked her what other things were going on, she explained that she had a new co-anchor and a new set. She was trying to adjust to both of these changes. It was also early spring and the air conditioning had not been turned up in the studio so she was uncomfortably hot every night. All of these factors combined to increase her stress level to the danger point.

Often the layers of stress come from events that happen outside the newsroom. These are the things that most of us think we should be able to handle without being affected by them. But events like a divorce, the death of a loved one, and illness are very real emotional factors that can create layers of stress for all of us. These events can be overwhelming for broadcasters who are already working in a chronic stress profession.

Panic attacks are a serious matter that cause a great deal of distress for many people. In fact, anxiety disorders affect more people than depression or substance abuse in this country. Luckily, there are professionals who can help with panic attacks and anxiety. I refer clients to psychologists and social workers who specialize in counseling people with these problems. Some medical doctors, specifically psychiatrists, may be helpful as well. But beware of any doctor who gives you prescription drugs alone to deal with the problem. Counseling usually helps you with the stress itself and doesn't just treat the symptoms as drugs do. (For help finding a specialist, see Chapter 8, Helpful Resources.)

How Stressed Are You?

The Holmes-Rahe Social Readjustment Ratings Scale[20] has been considered the best measurement of stress for over thirty years. It's a list of forty-one common stresses, both positive and negative, that we face in life.

Go through this list and circle the numbers next to any events that have happened in your life within the last twelve months. When you add these numbers, if your score is over 300 points you have a greatly increased chance of becoming ill from stress. A score of 150-299 reduces the risk by 30 percent, and a score of less than 150 gives you only a slight chance of illness. Of course, personality factors and lifestyle choices affect this as well.

Life Event	Points
Death of spouse	100
Divorce	73
Marital separation	65
Imprisonment	63
Death of close family member	63
Personal injury or illness	53

Marriage	50
Dismissal from work	47
Marital reconciliation	45
Retirement	45
Change in health of family member	44
Pregnancy	40
Sexual difficulties	39
Gain of new family member	39
Business readjustment	39
Change in financial state	38
Change in number of arguments with spouse	35
Major mortgage	32
Foreclosure of mortgage or loan	30
Change in responsibilities at work	29
Son or daughter leaving home	29
Trouble with in-laws	29
Outstanding personal achievement	28
Spouse begins or stops work	26
Begin or end school	26
Change in living conditions	25
Revision of personal habits	24
Trouble with boss	23
Change in work hours or conditions	20
Change in residence	20
Change in schools	20
Change in recreation	19
Change in church activities	19
Change in social activities	18
Minor mortgage or loan	17
Change in sleeping habits	16
Change in number of family reunions	15
Change in eating habits	15
Vacation	13
Christmas	12
Minor violation of the law	11

Scoring this scale for yourself should give you some insight into the level of stress that you're operating under right now. These stressors have a very significant effect on your life. Death of a spouse, for example, is so significant that ten times more people than others in their age group die during the first year after they have lost a spouse. And divorced persons have a twelve times higher illness rate during the first year after they are divorced.[21]

Recognizing the negative effects of too much stress should help you make the decision to deal with stress before it affects your life and health. It's not necessary for you to be a stress addict to perform well as a broadcaster. If you're already successful, it's who you are and your skills that got you there. If you're hoping to be successful in broadcasting, remember that adrenaline and stress never made anyone a success.

There's no doubt, however, that being too stressed has sabotaged many broadcasters' careers.

Healthy Suggestions

1 There are two areas of the body where most of us hold stress. The first is the face. The muscles of the jaw are some of the strongest in our bodies. Most of us clench our teeth at night or possibly even grind them. We wake up and continue to hold tension in this area. One way to relieve this tension throughout the day is to do some of the vocal exercises you'll find in Chapter 4. Performing vocal exercises several times a day will open your mouth and release the tension in your jaw.

It's also a good practice throughout the day to loosen your jaw slightly and rest the tip of your tongue on the ridge behind your upper front teeth (the alveolar ridge). This gives the jaw muscles a rest and helps focus your concentration on relaxing your mouth.

If you find that your jaw is very tight when you wake up every morning, you might want to investigate getting a nightguard to wear while you sleep. Dentists can fit you for one of these, and it will help you keep your jaw loose while you sleep. Most dentists feel a nightguard is a necessity if you tend to grind your teeth at night. Grinding erodes the surface of your teeth which can cause dental damage. I have had clients who are so stressed they even have to wear a nightguard at times during the day because they clench their teeth so tightly. Some have even cracked a tooth during the day because of clenching.

Another area of the body where we hold a lot of stress is in our stomach muscles. The armoring effect of the flight or fight response forces us to tighten our abdominal muscles for protection. Many of us hold these muscles tight during all our waking hours. This inhibits good abdominal-diaphragmatic breathing. We are forced to breathe in our upper chests which increases our stress level and affects our voice.

It's a good idea to develop a habit of focusing your attention on your abdomen several times every hour. When you feel that your stomach muscles are tense, consciously relax those muscles. Think, soft belly. (See Chapter 6 for proper abdominal-diaphragmatic breathing instructions and Healthy Suggestion #2 in that chapter for a discussion of softening your belly to relax.) This will help you let go of the tension in the abdominal area. Remember that we don't have to armor ourselves all the time. Sometimes our muscles can be soft.

2 Make a list of the ten things that make you the most stressed during an average day. These might include commuting in bad traffic, your spouse or kids, your news director, other people you work with, or equipment that malfunctions. Be specific. Once you have these ten things, draw a line down the page and next to each one brainstorm about ways you could relieve some of the stress.

No situation is so rigid that it is without options for improvement. Most of us think the stress in our lives is inevitable, but if we focus on what's bothering us, we can often improve it. One client of mine found that after doing this exercise he was able to completely transform his unpleasant commute. He discarded the newspapers he usually read in the car at every stoplight and began listening to books on tape. Then instead of switching madly from lane to lane and radio news station to radio news station, he was able to relax and enjoy his trip to work. He commented that he never noticed how beautiful the drive was until he made these changes.

3 Stress in the mind affects every cell in our body. You've read how your immune system and all your internal organs are eroded by stress. But the good news is that this is a two-way connection between the mind and the body.

Dr. Bernie Siegel says, "When we laugh every cell laughs."[22] Make time during each day to experience joy and laughter. This will help combat the ravages of stress. The little things you can do every day to make yourself happy and brighten the lives of those around you are really not so little after all (see Healthy Suggestion #1 in Chapter 2). A simple thing like giving someone a card or celebrating a birthday in the newsroom with cake and balloons can make a difference. Far from being a waste of time or frivolous, small breaks can be valuable stress-busters.

4 Vacation days are given for a reason. They help you rest and relax so that you can work at your peak performance. Only people who are not taking care of themselves amass days of unused vacation. At the beginning of each year, look over the calendar and plan your days off. It's a good idea to take at least one day off a month if possible.

It's also important to take off five days in a row or more at least once each year. When your body is very stressed, it may take a few days to come down from that stress. That's why many people feel lousy the first few days of their vacation. Taking a week or more off gives you time to unwind and enjoy your vacation time.

If you don't think vacation days are valuable for you, remember the last time you came back from some extended time off. Didn't you feel out of place in the newsroom and out of step? You may have wondered why everyone was so frantic. You may have felt a bit uncomfortable thinking that you had lost your edge. What you lost was your chronic stress, and you were very aware of it for a short time before you got back into the stress of your work environment. This should help you see that it's important to take time off to release as much stress as possible.

5 One of the most important things you can do to combat stress is to have balance in your life. This means that you have interests outside of work. I am constantly surprised when I ask a client to name a friend outside of work and that person cannot come up with one acquaintance who isn't in the business. If all of the people with whom you associate are in broadcasting, you have lost balance in your life.

Because of the frequency with which most broadcasters change jobs, it's often difficult to build relationships outside the newsroom. You may find yourself living in a new city and even a new part of the country every few years. You have to make a conscious effort to cultivate friends in other professions. Join health clubs or book clubs or a church or any group where you'll be in contact with other interesting people. This will help your stress level, and it will help you in your job. If you're reporting the news to the community, you need to know what that community is like. You won't know that if you limit your friends and acquaintances to other broadcasters.

Jot down the names of some of your friends who are not in the broadcasting business. If that list is short, you know your life is not as balanced as it should be. Think of ways that you can cultivate some new friends. This will mean, of course, that you will have to allow yourself time away from work to meet these people. But that's time you should be giving yourself anyway. Nothing will contribute to professional burn-out faster than overwork and isolation.

6 A good way to determine if you are addicted to stress is to note how often you watch or listen to the news when you're not working. If you are not assigned to work on the weekends, for example, you don't have to tune in to the news on Saturday and Sunday. You might feel you need to watch the late news Sunday night to become current on what has happened, but that may be enough. One client told me he can gauge his level of addiction to the stress of the news business by how difficult it is for him *not* to watch or listen to the news. He said he often tells himself he will watch for a couple of minutes and just catch the top stories. Hours later he finds he has watched the news on several stations instead of going out to do something else. He also finds it's difficult to listen to music on the radio in his car instead of the all-news station. Monitor yourself and note if you have difficulty *not* watching or listening to the news every time it's on.

Getting The Exercise You Need

From the Newsroom:

Donya Archer, Anchor/Reporter
WTXF-TV, Philadelphia, Pennsylvania

When I was twenty-one years old, I began my first broadcasting job. It was my initial experience working in the real world where my track record really mattered. I had big aspirations, and I wanted to do everything right even if that meant working 18 hours a day and checking everything 300 times to make sure it was correct. It seemed like there were not enough hours in the day to get everything done, and I had a tough time saying, "No," to extra assignments. So instead of leaving work to exercise, I would stay late. It got to the point where I was working so much and was so stressed out, I had gotten a pre-ulcer condition. I had to make a change. The stress level had gotten so bad that you could hear it in my voice. You could see it in my shoulders. You could see it on my face. When I held the mike, I would hang on with a death grip. If you came up behind me and put your finger on my shoulder, I would jump ten feet. I would barely recognize myself when I watched myself on the air. I was getting better at my job, no doubt, but I didn't look at ease. My personality wasn't able to come through because I was so nervous and tense about performing well. Finally, I forced myself to start running for some exercise, and then I joined a gym. I ended up doing weight training where I was able to get out some aggression. Now I exercise three or four times a week. I do aerobics, something I love, and dance. I mix that with yoga which is great for relaxation and getting yourself balanced. Some days I'll run. Some days I'll swim. I try to vary it so I don't get bored. It's important for me just to sweat and lose myself in something besides my job to clear my head. Exercising has become an integral part of my life, and I know it makes me better on the air. When I moved for my present job, I found my apartment and joined a gym so I could go work out right away. I feel like I'm mentally sharper when I'm exercising and keeping a regular schedule in general. I'm learning that if I lead a more balanced life, I'm a better anchor and reporter and a happier person. Spending 14 hours at the station trying to do everything I could when I wasn't running at an optimal pace wasn't productive or healthy. I still have times when I work long hours, but I'm better at knowing when to go and get the kinks out by exercising. If I were just beginning in the business, I would discipline myself to take at least an hour out of the day even two times a week just to go walk. Walking is not a lot of pressure. It's great exercise. You look around and have time to think about the things in life that are more important than deadlines and press conferences.

·4·

Getting The Exercise You Need

*The good news is that you don't really have to exercise
very much in order to get most of the health benefits.*
Dean Ornish, M.D.[1]

The votes are definitely in on the value of exercise, and it's hard to refute its benefits. But for most people working in broadcasting, exercise is a difficult thing to fit into an already overloaded schedule. When I mention exercise to most of my clients, they respond as one network bureau chief did, "Ann, you've got to be kidding! Unless you can add an extra hour to every day, exercise will never fit into my life."

In this chapter, you will see that exercise can fit into the busiest schedule. And you'll see that you don't have to become an Olympic athlete to benefit from exercise. I can vouch for that myself. I never did any regular aerobic exercise until I was almost forty years old. In fact, in school I was always the one with an excuse about why I couldn't go to physical education class. Growing up in the South taught me that ladies don't sweat, and exercise was the last thing I wanted to pursue. I followed that tradition for much of my life.

What I've discovered is that exercise is not as distasteful as I thought, and the benefits are enormous. Physically fit people show many positive health traits such as lower blood pressure, improved blood cholesterol, lower resting pulse rate, improved capability in dealing with stress, and higher immune function.[2] The benefits are so profound that Covert Bailey, one of our country's foremost health and fitness experts, jokes about a King Muscle pill.[3] If you take two after thirty minutes of aerobic exercise, you'll reap more health benefits than any pill ever invented. The pills are placebos. Obviously, exercise makes the difference.

Researchers now know that even a little physical exercise brings health improvements. One large research study showed that the greatest improvement occurs between the sedentary person and the one who performs moderate exercise.[4] And the same study showed that something as simple as walking thirty minutes a day reduced premature death almost as much as running thirty to forty miles per week. You don't have to go for the "burn" to get health benefits. For most people, a comfortable increase in heart rate is all that's needed (see Healthy Suggestion #1 to calculate your range of healthy heart rate). So you no longer have to think of exercise as separate from your daily life. It's not something for which you have to have expensive equipment or special clothes or something that takes a lot of time and effort. A little moderate exercise goes a long way.

What Is Aerobic Fitness?

Many people don't start an exercise program because it seems difficult to understand what needs to be done. It's really very simple. Aerobic fitness means that your body can efficiently extract oxygen from your blood and transport it to your muscles. Regular aerobic exercise increases the number of small blood vessels to the muscles which makes the exchange of oxygen and carbon dioxide more efficient. What you're trying to accomplish when you exercise aerobically is to make your body a better oxygen-using machine.

Our bodies are highly adaptable. If you lift weights with your arm every day, for example, your body will build more muscle to adjust to that behavior. If you wear shoes that are too small, your body will create an armoring system of calluses to protect your feet. Aerobic exercise causes an adaptation process by the body as well. When you continue to exercise on a regular basis, the body decides it's time to adapt to this increased heart rate by making your body more efficient. It's not the "killer" workout that causes this adaptation. It's the sustained aerobic exercise over time that does it. Your body decides that you're going to keep this up so it had better adapt by making you use oxygen more efficiently.

Most experts agree that for the most benefits you need to exercise at least twelve minutes in your target heart rate zone (See Healthy Suggestion #1) using big muscles in your body to reach the aerobic effect. Our big muscles are in our legs and buttocks. This aerobic period should be preceded by a warm-up of a few minutes to get your heart into the training zone and a cool-down at the end. Later in this chapter you'll find stretching exercises which can be a comfortable way to warm-up, or for both your warm-up and cool-down you can simply do your exercise at a slower speed.

When you combine the warm-up and cool-down with the aerobic exercise, it usually results in a thirty-minute workout. Doing this three or more times a week is ideal. But it doesn't even have to be done in a thirty-minute block. A study has shown that people who did three, ten-minute workouts with a short warm-up and cool-down each time spread out over the day showed significant benefits as well.[5] So the time factor can be adjusted to fit your schedule.

It's easy to remember the principle of exercise because it's not complicated. Do something that raises your heart rate moderately for a total of thirty minutes several times per week. What you do and where you do it are not too important. You can run in place, climb stairs, or work out on an expensive piece of exercise equipment. You can go to a health club or YMCA, exercise in your living room, or go up and down your stairs at work. You can walk on the beach, walk on a treadmill, or walk down the halls in a hotel. It's not rocket science. You just need to move for a sustained period of time as many times a week as possible.

Special Benefits of Exercise for Broadcasters

Nothing combats stress like exercise. That's important since stress is one of the most deadly aspects of working in the news business. In Chapter 3 we looked at the stress hormones and how they affect the body. With aerobic exercise, the body's stress hormone production is adjusted. When we begin an aerobic exercise program, the adrenal glands secrete lots of adrenaline. But as we continue the exercise over several months, our bodies get the message that they need to adjust the release of stress hormones. When this happens, it's nondiscriminatory. The body will release less when we exercise, and it will also release less when we have emotional stresses in our lives.[6]

Exercise can have a very real impact on your ability to deal with stress (See Figure 4.1). The TelePrompTer that malfunctions or the deadline that's sneaking closer won't seem as overwhelming when your body has adjusted physiologically to how it deals with stress.

The health benefits are equally as profound. The Centers for Disease Control and Prevention say that except for cigarette smoking, lack of exercise is the leading preventable cause of heart disease in the United States.[7] As an example, if

Figure 4.1 The effect of exercise on stress is summarized by exercise expert, Covert Bailey: The first 15 minutes you exercise you forget what you were upset with your boss about; the next 15 minutes you exercise you forget your boss' name; and the last 15 minutes, you forget you have a boss!

you have high blood pressure and exercise, you'll have a greater life expectancy than if you have normal blood pressure and don't exercise.[8]

But the benefits aren't limited to the cardiovascular system. For almost a hundred years scientists have known that regular, moderate exercise affects immunity. In recent years studies have shown that immune cells begin circulating through the body at a higher rate when a person performs regular aerobic exercise. The Cooper Institute for Aerobics Research found that regular exercise reduces your risk of death by disease by 60 percent.[9] This benefit alone should convince you to begin exercising.

If you're like most people, it's the very real illnesses like a common cold that you dread the most because they interfere with your career on a regular basis. Staying healthy and fit day to day is important when you work in broadcasting. Most of us ignore our cardiovascular health unless we've had a problem with it. Heart attacks seem like a remote risk. We want to stay healthy day to day. It's okay to exercise because you think it will help you avoid colds and other minor illnesses, but remember that exercise enhances your cardiovascular health enormously. That's important because more people — men and women — die from heart and blood vessel diseases each year than from all other causes of death *combined*.[10]

What Type of Exercise Works?

You can ignore the old "No Pain, No Gain" philosophy. Any pain in the body is a sign that something is wrong and should be listened to. Moderate aerobic exercise is all that you need to gain the health and longevity benefits. And always discuss your exercise plans with your doctor. This is especially important if:

- You are over forty years of age.
- You have a personal or family history of heart problems.
- You have any musculoskeletal weaknesses such as back, knee, or foot problems.
- You have any breathing problems.
- You are diabetic or have any other chronic health challenges.[11]

Clients often ask me if golf, softball, or basketball will work for their exercise needs. These activities are great fun and can help you stay fit, but it's the regular, nonstop sessions that are the most beneficial. Most of us can't indulge in competitive sports enough to get major benefits. Also basketball and team sports often require lots of stop and go action which works on the body in a different way. It may be anaerobic which means you exceed your training zone. Then your body begins to burn sugar instead of fat and the health effects are different. These sports may be something you want to do occasionally, but don't let them replace your steady aerobic workouts.

Also be aware that any group sport can become competitive which only adds to the stress in your life. That's the last thing you want to be doing. A client of mine began playing softball again after many years because he thought it would help his stress level. His lack of skill only increased his level of stress, and he sustained some injuries. He found he needed to get in better shape before he went on the ball field. And he had to remember that he wasn't the same athlete he had been in college.

I can confirm that any exercise can become competitive. I took yoga classes for over twenty years, but I had to stop because I became so competitive. Here's an activity that should be very relaxing, but I couldn't control my desire to be the best in the class. Now I do yoga alone, and I don't have the pulled muscles and stress that I caused for myself when taking classes. So any activity can become stressful. Remember that you don't have to run the farthest, work out the longest, or be the best at aerobic exercise. You just have to keep it up at a moderate level week in and week out.

The Health Benefits of Exercise

Dean Ornish, a physician who has documented that heart disease can be halted and even reversed with lifestyle changes such as exercise, outlines the health benefits of aerobic exercise as follows:

- Increases bone density
- Decreases formation of blood clots
- Raises levels of HDL ("good") cholesterol
- Lowers triglycerides
- Reduces body fat
- Supplies more blood and oxygen to the muscles
- Lowers blood pressure
- Improves strength and flexibility.[12]

These benefits are not always immediately observable, but I see the following changes in my clients:

- Less anxiety
- Improved methods for coping with daily stressors
- Less insomnia
- Increased energy level
- Better self-esteem
- Relief from depression
- Positive body image.

Both health and emotional benefits can be the results of any regular aerobic exercise plan. One television producer is a

clear example of how exercise helps both physically and emotionally. This woman was working at a station that was
undergoing management changes. The feeling was that no
one's job was safe. She began to suffer from arthritis attacks
where her joints would become swollen. It got so bad that she
ended up on crutches. She spoke with me about her plight,
and realized that the stress was killing her. "Silly me," she
said, "This work is important to me, but it's not my whole
life." She decided to take some days off and begin to take care
of herself. Up until that time, she had been saving her sick
leave and vacation days because she thought she would need
the income from them if she was laid off. But she was pushing
herself at exactly the time when she needed to relax.

When this producer began exercising, she told me she
could barely walk down her driveway and back, but she
persevered. Slowly she began walking for longer distances.
Finally she was able to jog which she had done years before.
It wasn't a fast change, but after several months, she was
feeling healthy. Her arthritis improved, and she was able to
deal with her work stresses in a better way. She found that
as long as she kept up with her exercise, she didn't have any
relapses. Taking some time off with an exercise plan and at-
tacking her stress level and the health challenges it had created, turned her life around.

Common Excuses

The most common excuse I hear not to exercise is, "I
simply don't have the time." This comment is often followed by, "When I do have some free time, I want to do
something fun." Let's look at the first part of this response.
When you break exercise down into three, ten-minute periods a day, it's really not hard to find the time. Let me give
some examples of what can fill that ten minutes:

- Walking outside around the building at work.
- Climbing a few flights of stairs at home, work, or on your way to an appointment.
- Taking a walk while you eat lunch (you're not increasing your heart rate to the point that it's dangerous to combine light eating and exercise).
- Doing a short workout on a piece of exercise equipment while you watch TV or read a magazine or newspaper.
- Taking a walk around the halls if you work in a large building or are staying at a hotel.
- Parking farther from your destination and walking the remaining distance.

These are just some examples of types of exercise you can do in ten minutes. Of course, most of these can be extended to thirty minutes as well.

If you feel you don't have time, take a close look at your day. Most of us have time that we can adjust. Also, most of us find time to do things that are a priority for us. Hopefully, knowing more about exercise will help make it a priority for you.

But what about the people who want to do something fun with the little free time they have? Well, many forms of aerobic exercise are fun. You can dance, swim, or walk with a friend or loved one. You might find it's fun to take an aerobics class or jog with a friend. There's nothing that says aerobic exercise has to be punishment.

There's one more important thing to keep in mind when you think you don't have time to exercise. Often getting up for a short exercise break will give you the ability to accomplish tasks more quickly and more efficiently. Continuing to push all through your day can backfire on you. You may become less efficient. And if you're an on-air talent, your performance will definitely suffer when this happens. Like many things about taking care of yourself as a broadcaster, an exercise break is not a luxury. It's a necessity.

Another common excuse is that it's too inconvenient to go to a health club or gym. When it comes to exercising, what works for people really varies. Many love the camaraderie of working out with other people. Others like to make exercise a personal time. If you love a gym, you'll usually find time to go there. But there are other options. One of the best investments you can make is to buy a piece of exercise equipment to have at home. That way you can exercise any time of day or night and in any kind of weather. It doesn't matter if you buy a treadmill, stationary bicycle, ski machine, or any of the other kinds of equipment that are available. As long as you're comfortable doing it, and the equipment uses your large muscles, it's fine. This equipment combined with the other suggestions of ways to get exercise given above will help you achieve your goal of working out on a regular basis.

Another option is for your station to provide a workout area. WUSA-TV in Washington, D.C., has done exactly that. They have a well-outfitted exercise room with free weights and gym equipment right in the building. This gives employees an opportunity to stop in for exercise during the day. This is a small investment of money that can reap major returns in the health and performance of employees. Corporations such as Hewlett Packard and Xerox have found that it is cost effective to provide fitness rooms and wellness programs for their employees. News organizations should consider this as well.

Another common excuse not to exercise is, "I'm too out of shape. There's no hope for me." Well, there's hope for everyone. Even nursing home residents in their eighties and nineties have benefited from moderate exercise. And as you read earlier in this chapter, it's going from being sedentary to moderate exercise that gives the greatest benefits. Even if you begin by walking around your desk, you'll be better off.

I also have clients who tell me that they want to spend time with their children when they get home. Well, why not work out with them? Children love being active. In addition, by making exercise a priority, you're modeling behavior for them that will change their lives. They'll grow up seeing the importance of staying physically fit. You can begin this early. Even an infant can be pushed in a stroller while you walk. As children get older, they can participate in your exercise right along with you.

The Benefits of Stretching

A mild and enjoyable type of exercise that you can do several times throughout your day is stretching. This can be done anywhere with no special equipment. It can be done solely for its benefits or as a warm-up for a longer aerobic workout.

We have over 600 skeletal muscles in our body, and each of these muscles can hold tension. Stopping to stretch these muscles all through the day will keep tension from building up in the body.

Let's look at a typical reporter and see how tension might affect her. She might clench her teeth while sleeping, producing tightness in her jaw and face. She might hold tension in her forehead as she speeds to her first location for a story. Her leg muscles might get tense while she stands waiting for an interview. Back in the newsroom she may suffer shoulder and neck cramps while she writes at her computer. All of these muscles can hold residual tension. Combine the tension held by them, and you have a very tense body.

Stretching offers two benefits. First, it releases tension in the muscles that are being stretched. Secondly, it focuses your attention on the stretching which momentarily takes your attention away from what is stressing you. This little mental break will help you relax while getting the benefit of the actual stretching.

There's a right way and a wrong way to stretch. Nothing will pull a tensed muscle faster than a quick, jerky movement. You should avoid bouncing, jerking, swinging, or anything that causes pain. Proper stretching is done with your breathing, in a relaxed way. Your attention should be on the muscles you're stretching so that you don't move in a way that is painful. And you don't have to be the most limber person around. That can get you in trouble just as I got in trouble when I made my yoga classes competitive and began hurting myself. Stretching should be relaxed and peaceful, and it should only go to the point of resistance, no further.

And because stretching is so simple, it can be integrated into your day on many occasions. Here are some times you might think of stretching:

- When you first awaken. You can stretch while you're still in bed.
- Once you get out of bed.
- After your bath or shower.
- After standing a long time.
- After sitting a long time.
- After long telephone conversations.
- Every fifteen minutes when doing computer input or editing.
- Before an aerobic workout.
- Before on-air work if you're a reporter or anchor.
- Before you leave work to commute home.
- At home in the evening.

Many stretches work well at any of these times. Here is a series of stretches that can be done separately or as a sequence. You can perform the entire series in less than five minutes. But you can also pick out a single stretch that might feel especially good, like shoulder rolls after working at a computer, and do that alone.

Do all these stretches in a standing position with your knees slightly flexed and your feet apart about as wide as your shoulders. Remember not to bounce or throw your body into a stretch. If you have any pain, do not do the stretching and check with your physician.

1. Begin with your hands at your sides. Raise your hands above your head in a slow stretch. Reach up several times as if you are trying to pick apples just above your reach. Lower your arms. Repeat four times.

2. Interlace your fingers with your hands behind your head and your elbows out to your sides. Stretch up and back drawing your shoulder blades toward each other and gently arching your back. Stretch your elbows forward as if trying to touch them together. Let them drop down toward the floor, and gently pull your head down toward your chest. Repeat gently in a flowing manner four times.

3. Pretend you are swimming using the breaststroke. Begin with your arms straight out in front of you with the backs of your hands touching. Stroke back as far as you can comfortably with both arms. Repeat four times.

4. Pretend you are swimming using the backstroke. With the same beginning position as #2 or #3, rotate one arm back and follow your hand with your eyes. Repeat with the other arm. Begin again. Repeat four times with each arm.

5. Interlace your fingers behind you with your arms straight. Begin with your face forward and your chin level with the floor. Slowly lift your arms up behind you as far as you can go until you feel a comfortable stretch. As you lift let your head stretch upward. (Be careful not to let the head fall backward since this can injure the neck.) Hold the stretch for five seconds. Repeat four times.

6. Roll your shoulders slowly moving both at the
    same time. Begin by pulling them up toward your
    ears. From this position, rotate them back so that
    your shoulder blades are coming together. Now
    stretch them down. Finish by rotating them for-
    ward as if trying to make your shoulders touch in
    front. Continue this rotating four times. Change di-
    rection and rotate four times.

The Benefits of Vocal Exercises

There's one more type of exercise that is important for
broadcasters, especially if they are on-air. Vocal exercises
should be a part of every on-air person's day. They are also
helpful for the rest of us because they relax the vocal mechanism and the face and neck. In my book, *Broadcast Voice
Handbook*, I give the example that no runner would walk
out the door and immediately begin running a marathon.
You've learned this about any aerobic exercise as you've
read this chapter. Before exercise we need to warm-up our
muscles to make them work more efficiently. Our vocal
muscles need to be warmed-up in order to work efficiently
as well.

Muscles are an integral part of our vocal mechanism as
you read in Chapter 2. The jaw is operated by very strong
muscles that we use for chewing. The vocal folds are ligaments and muscle in our throat. The tongue is a large muscle in the mouth that extends down our pharynx. All these
muscles benefit from being exercised and stretched. Good
speech requires that they be agile to articulate our sounds
well.

I always encourage clients to do vocal exercises even if
they are the only one in their newsroom doing them. Other
professionals like singers, actors, dancers, and athletes
know that they need to warm-up before they begin their

work. By doing vocal warm-ups they are showing their professionalism and their respect for their instrument which is their body. Broadcasters should show the same level of professionalism.

Warming up the voice is easy and doesn't take a lot of time to see benefits. Here are some warm-ups taken from *Broadcast Voice Handbook*. Make them part of your daily routine if you are on-air or if you simply want your voice to sound better.

1) Say these phonemes (sounds), exaggerating the mouth positions:
   - /ɑ/ as in spa
   - /ɔ/ as in caw
   - /u/ as in two
   - /i/ as in bee

   Open the mouth wide for /ɑ/, round the lips for /ɔ/, pull the lips forward in a pucker for the /u/ phoneme, and smile widely for /i/. Continue to say these phonemes in an exaggerated manner, gliding from one to the next. Use this series of phonemes as a warm-up before going on air. After repeating them a dozen times or more in an exaggerated manner you should feel your mouth becoming more flexible.

2) Continuing with the exaggerated stretching found in the last warm-up, repeat this sentence extending the vowel phonemes:
   - You see Oz.

   Pucker the lips tightly for "you." Pull the lips back in a wide smile for "see," and drop the jaw and open wide for "Oz." Repeat this sentence with these exaggerated lip positions as many times as you need to in order to warm-up your articulators.

3) Repeat the following sentences as fast as you can while preserving the articulation of the ending t's, p's, and k's:

- Put a cup. Put a cup. Put a cup. Put a cup.
- Drink buttermilk. Drink buttermilk. Drink buttermilk.

Rapid repetition of these sentences will help warm-up your tongue. Say these sentences rapidly before on-air work. Be sure you feel air exploding out on the t's, p's, and k's.

4) Chewing and talking at the same time has been used extensively to improve articulation because chewing loosens the jaw and tongue. To practice this, pretend you have just taken a big bite from an apple and count while you chew. You can also say the months of the year, days of the week, or the alphabet to experience this warm-up. You should exaggerate your chewing while you speak.

Healthy Suggestions

1 To get the most benefits from exercise, be sure to stay within the healthy limits that define aerobic exercise for you. This is called your target heart rate zone. If you exercise below your target heart rate, you don't get all the benefits exercise can offer. If you go above your target heart rate you move into the anaerobic zone which works your body in a different manner.

To calculate your target heart rate, do this calculation:

Subtract your age from 220

$$220$$
$$-\underline{\qquad} \text{(your age)}$$

Your maximum safe
heart rate

$$\underline{\qquad}$$

Multiply your maximum
heart rate by .50

(maximum rate)

$$\times .50$$

The low end of your
target range

$$\underline{\qquad}$$

Multiply your maximum
heart rate by .80

(maximum rate)

$$\times .80$$

The high end of your
target range

$$\underline{\qquad}$$

Take your pulse several times while you exercise to see if you are in your target heart rate zone. If you're just beginning an exercise program, you might want to work at the low end of your target range for a while. Once you are more fit, you can move toward the high end of your range. But stay within your target heart rate zone for best results. Remember that moderate exercise is what you want. You will not get the benefits of moderate exercise if you move higher than 80 percent of your maximum heart rate.

You can take your pulse by pressing lightly with the index and middle finger of one hand on the radial artery (just below the thumb on your wrist) of the other arm. Don't use your thumb to take your pulse since the thumb has its own pulse which may result in an inaccurate reading. Or you may prefer using your index and middle finger to feel your carotid artery which is in your neck straight down from the outer corner of your eye below your chin.

To make checking your pulse easier, you might want to calculate your 10-second count by dividing your minimum and maximum target heart rate zones by 6. This will allow you to count your pulse for 10 seconds and know if you are in your target zone. Keep your minimum and maximum 10-second numbers memorized, and you'll be able to quickly calculate how hard you're working.

When exercising always monitor your level of exertion. Check your pulse often and don't overexert yourself. Signs to watch for are feeling dizzy or extremely winded, pounding or discomfort in your chest, or sweating more than usual. In any of these instances, stop exercising and consult a doctor if the symptoms persist.

2 There are a couple of things you can do that will help you begin an exercise plan and stick with it. Get in touch with what excuses you're using not to

exercise and also tell yourself what personal benefits exercise has for you. Fill in the following lists to help you in this process:

Common Excuses I Use To Avoid Exercise:

1. _____

2. _____

3. _____

Now go back to the section of this chapter that deals with common excuses and see if there are ways to navigate around your excuses.

Reasons I Want To Exercise:

1. _____

2. _____

3. _____

Hopefully, you will be able to think of more than just these three reasons why you want to exercise!

3 If you feel you would like some assistance with your exercise plan, there are professionals who can be very helpful. Your doctor may be able to help you design an exercise plan. A cardiologist can assist you in determining a healthy exercise plan by giving you a treadmill exercise test that includes both a resting and exercising electrocardiogram and blood pressure measurements. This is especially important if you have a family or personal history of cardiovascular problems.

You can also get help designing an exercise plan from a personal trainer. Trainers are employed by most health clubs and fitness centers and are often at your local YMCA. It's good to inquire about the certification that any trainer has. A trainer should be certified either by the American Council on Exercise (ACE), the American College of Sports Medicine, or another reputable group.

Many personal trainers can come directly to you to help you design a program and stay with it. This is a small investment of money when you consider the benefits of knowing that you are doing the best exercise for your particular body. If you're planning to buy some exercise equipment, you might want to contact a personal trainer first. He or she can help you get the best equipment at the best price. To find a personal trainer in your area who is certified by the American Council on Exercise, call ACE at 800-529-8227. The Fitness Connection (800-318-4024) is another helpful resource that can arrange to send a personal trainer to your home or anywhere you might be traveling.

5

Getting the Nutrition You Need

From the Newsroom:

Page Hopkins, Anchor/Reporter
News 12 New Jersey

I ate very poorly when I started reporting. I was a junkaholic. I ate lots of fast food, and as a result I was having stomach and intestinal problems. My hair even started falling out. Every morning I would eat sugared cereal with milk and find myself tired for a couple of hours afterwards. I was feeling cloudy and foggy because of the sugar, and what would I do to cure it? I would have a Snickers and a diet Coke. The worst possible thing I could eat. And I wondered why my hair was falling out! I realized how important food was when I started looking at tapes of myself. I could tell the days when I wasn't eating well. I could see subtle things like a lack of focus when I looked at the camera or a slower rate. I listened to how differently my voice sounded when I was eating well and drinking lots of water. For example, when I go on air to anchor at ten o'clock, if I haven't had a certain amount of protein throughout the day, I'm not able to think as clearly. I'm just not as quick on the uptake. I finally made the connection between eating protein and thinking. When you're an anchor in the studio all day, you can pretty much control what you're going to eat. You can bring your lunch and dinner. It's much harder when you're out reporting. If you're getting ready for a live shot, and you have a half-hour for dinner, sometimes there's only McDonald's or a greasy spoon. In that situation, I have to make a conscious effort to order a baked potato and a salad. Sometimes it's very hard when I'm crashing and my sugar levels are dropping. All I want to do is wrap my lips around a cheeseburger and fries and a milk shake like the camera person might be doing. But I have to be very disciplined. Ultimately, I know I'm going to feel better and be on top of my story because I'm more mentally present. This business is so physical and your body is really your instrument. What you eat is very important because it affects everything. You have to be very vigilant about what you eat and how frequently you eat. I've pointed this out to friends when they complain about a live shot or package they've done. I'll ask them, "Did you eat?" And they'll say, "Well, I had a blueberry muffin at 9 this morning." This live shot might be at 5:00 p.m. That's not enough fuel to keep a person's body running. You have to eat and drink lots of water throughout the day. I finally made the connection between my performance and eating, and there is a critical connection there. It means I have to plan ahead and bring healthy food with me every day, but it's worth it.

Getting the Nutrition You Need

*If we are what we eat, then from 9 to 5 many of us are
either bottomless cups of coffee or the
F9 button on the candy machine.*
Francine Hermelin[1]

Seneca, a Roman philosopher who lived nearly two thousand years ago, said, "We dig our graves with our teeth."[2] This is no exaggeration. And in broadcasting, that statement can be expanded to say we increase our stress level and sabotage our performance when we aren't eating well. One female network television anchor pointed out that there isn't enough make-up in the world to cover two margaritas the night before.

An avalanche of material about nutrition and diet comes out every month. There's so much material that you may feel overwhelmed by it and decide to ignore it all. If you do, you're not alone. Most of my clients say they don't have time to think about what they eat. And many times they don't even have time to eat. Numerous broadcasters have told me they grab a quick breakfast that includes a couple of cups of coffee. They leave for the station, and food doesn't enter their minds (or their mouths) again until they return home eight, ten, or even twelve hours later. They keep going on caffeine. For these people, studying the trends in nutrition is the last thing they have time to do.

Fortunately, improving your diet is not as complicated as it seems, and the payoff is enormous. Eating right will give you energy, help your mind function better, and help you stay well. Food is more powerful than any drug your doctor could prescribe.[3] Dr. Christine Northrup says, "Eating healthy, high-quality food is one of the easiest and most powerful ways to create health on a daily basis."[4]

What does food give us? It gives us proteins, minerals, and water, all of which help our bodies grow and repair themselves and sustain our body structures. We also get vitamins that combine with proteins, minerals, and water to keep our internal processes working effectively. Proteins, fats, and carbohydrates provide energy and maintain our body temperature. In short, food keeps our bodies running.

Poor nutrition stresses our bodies and our minds. This compounds the stresses that are a normal part of working in broadcasting (see Chapter 2). Also, when we're stressed, our nutritional needs increase. Apply this to broadcasting, and you see that at a time when we need good nutrition the most because of the stresses of the business, those same stresses may force us to ignore our eating habits. This is a vicious cycle that affects our health and work performance every day.

Improving Your Diet

There are a few important areas concerning diet that I find are challenges for most broadcasters. Making some changes in these areas does not require a Ph.D. in nutrition. Anyone can understand them.

Developing some healthy eating habits won't mean you're going to feel deprived either. To improve your diet, you will have to do as Florence Griffith Joyner suggests, "Stay away from the f-words: fried foods, fatty foods, and fast foods."[5] But there are plenty of healthy food choices that taste great. It's not hard to make these choices. Ordering a baked potato instead of french fries, for example, will give you half the calories and ten times less fat. That's a simple change that can make a big difference.

For broadcasters there are three important nutrition areas to consider. You must eat enough, stay away from the wrong foods, and drink plenty of water.

Getting the Nutrition You Need

Consuming less than 1800 calories a day is a risk factor for low-nutrient intake.[6] Your body needs over forty different nutrients to stay healthy.[7] Eating too little puts you at risk because you don't have the variety of foods or the calorie intake to supply these nutrients.

A survey by the Cooper Institute for Aerobics Research reported that at any given time 50 percent of American women and 25 percent of men say they are on a diet.[8] Less than 1 percent of the population has full-blown anorexia nervosa, but severely limiting calories is much more common. From my experience, this is especially a problem for on-air television broadcasters. Many tell me they must starve themselves to stay as thin as they think they need to be for television.

Starving yourself is like asking your car to run with a few drops of gasoline in the tank. If you run your car until it's that empty, the car's performance will suffer. It will sputter and lose acceleration. Our bodies work the same way. With too little food and too many hours between eating, we stumble through the day. You may have come to accept your daily bouts of fatigue, but what may be happening is that your food tank is on empty. If you're especially stressed or busy, you might not even feel hungry. But when your blood sugar level drops, your body suffers.

Blood sugar levels should stay between 70 and 100 milligrams. When they drop below 70 mg, your visual acuity is affected. You may have trouble focusing on your computer screen or the lights in the room may seem dimmer. Your brain uses over 70 percent of the glucose that is in your body, so when your blood sugar drops below 60 mg your short-term memory will be affected. Below 50 mg and you become irritable and can't take in new information as efficiently.[9] When you go more than four hours without food, your blood sugar drops low enough to cause fatigue and possibly some of the problems associated with low blood sugar.[10]

Low blood sugar also signals a sort of emergency for the body and tells it to get some food in fast. This may result in reaching for the foods that contribute to stress like caffeine or sugar. As you will read later, these foods give you an immediate burst of sugar in your system which can have unhealthy results. You may also tend to eat too much once you feel the emergency alarm go off. If you don't eat all day, you may not notice hunger until after your work day is over. Then you may eat a very big meal late at night which is the worst time of the day to eat a large quantity of food.

You should finish eating at least two hours before you go to bed. Too much food late at night will affect your ability to sleep well (see Chapter 7) and can cause a condition called gastric reflux. This condition is caused by undigested food in the stomach when you are in a prone position. Some of the stomach acid may come up the esophagus into the throat causing irritation the next day and possible hoarseness and discomfort when speaking. Eating fatty foods close to bedtime is especially bad since they take up to five to seven hours to digest. Fruit, on the other hand, takes less than an hour, and bread only one to three hours. If you must eat close to bedtime, make it a light, low fat meal.

A time when you do want to eat is at breakfast. Too many people ignore the importance of starting the day with food. After a long dietary fast during the hours you're sleeping, it's important to raise your blood sugar level with something healthy. This doesn't mean two cups of coffee and a doughnut. What you need is some protein, carbohydrates, and a little fat. If you feel you have to, include a cup or two of coffee.

Why are protein, carbohydrates, and fat important? Basically, they are the building blocks that our bodies need. You should aim to balance each meal and snack:

Balanced Meals and Snacks
- one-third protein
- two-thirds carbohydrates
- and a small amount of fat

Protein

Every cell in our body contains some protein. Excluding water, our body weight is 50 percent protein.[11] Protein builds tissue, including muscle. It also keeps our immune systems functioning, carries nutrients through our bodies, and helps enzyme reactions like digestion take place.[12] It's essential to a healthy body.

If you eat too little food during the day, your body will begin to use protein to do what carbohydrates and fat usually do, which is to supply energy. The first order of business in our bodies is always to stoke the engine with fuel. This energy to keep us going is more important than tissue rebuilding and the other functions protein should carry out. So when protein has to give up its usual jobs of keeping our immune system healthy, building new tissue, and helping our bodily functions run smoothly, we run the risk of getting sick.

Where do we get protein? Meat is, of course, a good source, but it is also often high in fat content. Here is a list of some protein sources:

Protein Content

	Amount of food	Amount of protein
Beef, lean ground	3 ounces cooked	23.4 grams
Cheddar Cheese	1 ounce	7.1 grams
Cottage Cheese	1/2 cup	15 grams
Eggs	2 medium	11.4 grams
Skim Milk	1 cup	8.8 grams
Peanut Butter	2 tablespoons	8 grams
Tuna, canned	3 ounces drained	24.4 grams
Turkey	3 ounces	26.8
Yogurt	1 cup	8.3[13]

Carbohydrates

Carbohydrates play an important role in our daily life. Complex carbohydrates actually boost our metabolic rate, which speeds up digestion and increases our energy level. The key is to get enough complex carbohydrates.

Carbohydrates are classified as simple and complex. Simple ones are sugars like honey, table sugar, and alcohol. These are empty calories without any nutritional value. Complex carbohydrates are made up of chains of sugars and provide lots of nutritional value. These include foods such as potatoes, bread, pasta, and rice. They provide long-lasting sources of energy for our bodies. Here is a sample of healthy complex carbohydrates taken from the hundreds you have to choose from[14]:

Carbohydrate Contents

	Amount of food	Amount of carbohydrates
Apple	1 large	27.3 grams
Banana	1 large	44.4 grams
Whole Wheat Bread	1 slice	11.3 grams
Corn Flakes	1 cup	21 grams
Oatmeal	1 cup	26 grams

Grapes	1 cup	18.5 grams
Orange juice	1 cup	27 grams
Mixed green salad	1 cup	9.6 grams
Potato, baked	1 large	36 grams
Rice, brown	1 cup	43 grams
Spaghetti		
(no sauce)	1 cup	44.1 grams

Fat

Most of us fear eating too much fat because we know eating fat can make us fat. But the real threat with fat intake is the effect on the heart and circulatory system. Saturated fat raises blood cholesterol levels in many people and increases the risk of heart disease. Saturated fat is the main type of fat that can give us significant health problems. Saturated fats are found in largest amounts in meat and dairy products and in some oils like coconut, palm, and palm kernel. Keep your intake from these sources of fat as low as possible.

Monounsaturated and polyunsaturated fats actually reduce blood cholesterol. Most of the fat we eat should come from these types. Monounsaturated fats are found mainly in olive, peanut, and canola oils. Polyunsaturated fats are found in safflower, sunflower, corn, soybean oils, and some fish.

The U.S. Department of Agriculture Dietary Guidelines recommend that Americans limit fat in their diets to 30 percent of their total calories. Monounsaturated and polyunsaturated fats should comprise the largest part of that percentage. Other authorities such as cardiologist Dr. Dean Ornish like to reduce total fat intake to 10 percent. That's sometimes difficult to do. For most of us, if we make choices that are low-fat such as skim milk instead of whole milk and fish instead of red meat, we probably will be in an appropriate percentage area. If you have any cardiovascular problems or high cholesterol, you should, of course, follow your physician's recommendation.

Ignoring the fat content in foods, you can easily exceed the 30 percent that's recommended. For example, a bologna and cheese sandwich with mayonnaise weighs in at 36 grams of fat. If you're on an 1800 calorie diet, that's over half the 60 grams of fat you need for an entire day.[15] (See Healthy Suggestion #8 for an easy way to calculate fat percentage.)

Even worse than that are some snacks. If you haven't eaten in hours, and you smell an enticing Cinnabon odor at a mall, you may think it can't hurt too much to indulge. But a Cinnabon has 670 calories and as much fat as a Big Mac plus a hot fudge sundae. A Mrs. Fields Double Fudge Brownie has 420 calories and as much fat as two slices of Domino's Extra Cheese and Pepperoni Pizza with an additional two pats of butter on top![16] So a little slip can make a big difference. Here is a sample of some additional fat contents[17]:

Fat Content

	Amount of food	Amount of fat
Bread	1 slice	1 gram
Croissant	1 large	12 grams
Doughnut	1 medium	11 grams
Cake, frosted	1 slice	13 grams
French fries	10	8 grams
Skim milk	1 cup	trace
Whole milk	1 cup	8 grams
Cheddar Cheese	1 1/2 ounces	14 grams
Ground beef lean	3 ounces	16 grams
Nuts	1/3 cup	22 grams
Mayonnaise	1 tablespoon	11 grams
Cream Cheese	1 ounce	10 grams
Chocolate bar	1 ounce	9 grams

The Food Pyramid

In 1992 the U.S.D.A. designed a new model to illustrate what a healthy diet should look like. Using this model, you can construct a diet that meets the requirements of protein, carbohydrates, and a little fat with each meal (see Figure 5.1).

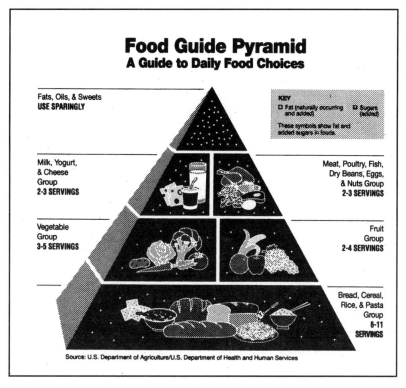

Figure 5.1 Recommended daily servings of each food group.

When looking at this chart, remember that no food group is more important than another. The differences are just in the quantities. For good health we need to eat the recommended amount of foods from each area. The combination gives us the nutrients we need each day. (The U.S.D.A. also offers helpful brochures that give more information about good nutrition. See Chapter 8, Helpful Resources.)

Grazing

You may wonder how you could possibly find the time to eat all these foods. A career in broadcasting doesn't provide a chance to sit and carefully plan your meals every day. You have to eat on the run most of the time. The way to solve this dilemma is to graze. Grazing means eating five small meals a day. This is recommended by many nutritionists because it helps you avoid the drop in blood sugar that comes if you go more than four hours without eating.

When you graze, your eating schedule might look something like this:

Eating Schedule
Breakfast
Lunch
Afternoon Snack
Dinner
Evening Snack

If you find you have a long time between breakfast and lunch, you might want to move your evening snack up there. The main objective is to eat every four hours, especially during your busiest work times. These snacks that are included are not just to stave off hunger. They are to give you the energy you need and to keep your blood sugar elevated so that you perform at the best of your ability.

I hear complaints all the time from clients about how their energy drops just before air-time if they are evening anchors. Or some producers tell me they get a headache every day around four o'clock. These are often signs of low blood sugar combined with stress. Eating regularly will help stop these periods of pain and poor performance. Think of your food intake as the equivalent of taking a medication every four hours to avoid the physical symptoms of low blood sugar.

If you follow the advice given with the pyramid, you can put together healthy meals and snacks that you can eat in the newsroom or out in the field. You should pack an emergency food kit in your bag every day and keep an air-tight container of foods in your desk. Make it a practice to take three pieces of fresh fruit with you every day. If you have to eat from a fast-food restaurant or a vending machine, make healthy choices. Most restaurants offer baked potatoes, salads, and orange juice or skim milk. And vending machines may include yogurt, apples, raisins, peanuts, and low-fat granola bars. A simple choice of peanuts instead of cheese crackers with peanut butter will save you fat and calories.

Having healthy snacks available at home and at work will help improve your diet. If you tend to turn to food to unwind and calm yourself down, it's especially important to shop wisely. Dr. Christine Northrup points out that it's hard to eat eight apples when you're upset or starving, but three pieces of cheesecake go down quite well.[18] So stock your cabinets, desk, and refrigerator with healthy choices.

You may think it's hard to find foods that will fit your busy lifestyle. I often advise that clients go to a grocery (preferably one that focuses on healthy, whole foods) and buy some of the following items. These are great carbohydrates for snacks or meals and can be carried easily:

Healthy Carbohydrate Snacks
 Apples
 Grapes
 Bananas
 Snack boxes of raisins
 Juice boxes that contain 100 percent fruit juice
 Carrot or celery sticks
 Snack-packs of canned fruit in juice (not in heavy
  syrup)
 Snack-packs of applesauce

> Dried fruits
> Vegetable juice in small cans (preferably low salt)
> Whole grain breads and crackers
> Pita bread
> Bagels (whole wheat)
> Bread sticks
> Cereal boxes in one-serving size
> Instant oatmeal in single serving packets
> No-salt pretzels
> Animal crackers

Combining these carbohydrate snacks with protein will give you what you need for energy. You should aim for the one-third protein, two-thirds carbohydrate ratio in every meal and snack. Here are some protein suggestions that can be combined with the foods listed above:

> **Protein to Add to Snacks**
> Low-fat cheese
> Low-fat milk
> Low-fat cottage cheese
> Low-fat yogurt
> Tuna or salmon canned (preferably in water)
> Slice of turkey or chicken
> Sardines canned in water (preferably low salt)
> Natural peanut butter (limit this to 2 tablespoons)

In the newsroom, rely on the refrigerator and microwave to fix meals that are fast and easy. Keep baking potatoes in your desk. They are nutritious, and can be topped with low-fat cottage cheese or low-fat cheese slices. Instant lentil or noodle soup cups are easy and healthy. Low-fat yogurt and fruit can be combined with a whole wheat bagel and low-fat cream cheese for a quick meal.

Instead of pizza or a dinner of candy and crackers from the vending machine, plan ahead. Stock low-fat yogurt, cheese, and cottage cheese in the newsroom refrigerator. Keep some whole wheat bread choices (crackers, bread, bagels), instant oatmeal, soups, and potatoes in your desk, and you'll never have to turn to unhealthy choices in a pinch. This doesn't take much planning. With one shopping trip you can stock up for several weeks.

Staying Away From the Wrong Foods

Grazing will not help you if you eat the wrong foods at these times. Coffee and a doughnut will hurt your energy level, not help it.

Caffeine

More than half the world's coffee is consumed in the United States.[19] I sometimes think about half of that coffee is brewing in newsrooms. I asked one television client how much coffee he drank every day, and I thought I heard him wrong when he responded. He told me he routinely consumed three to four *pots* of coffee a day. He wasn't kidding.

But even if he had told me three or four cups a day, he would still be over the healthy limit. The American Medical Association recommends no more than 200 milligrams of caffeine per day. Anything over 200 mg (around two cups of coffee) causes extra adrenaline to be pumped into the body. 200 to 400 mg of coffee may increase adrenaline 200 percent and elevate respiratory rate 20 percent.[20]

Caffeine is a substance that chemically stimulates the body's nervous system. And caffeine comes in all kinds of drinks, candies, and medications. Here's a partial list that shows caffeine content:

Caffeine Content of Beverages, Foods, and Common Drugs[21]

Beverages	Average milligrams of caffeine
Coffee (5-oz. cup)	
Brewed, drip method	115
Brewed, percolator	80
Instant	65
Decaffeinated, brewed	3
Decaffeinated, instant	2
Tea (5-oz. cup)	
Brewed, major U.S. brands	40
Brewed, imported brands	60
Instant	30
Iced (12-oz. glass)	70
Cocoa beverage (5-oz. cup)	4
Chocolate milk beverage (8 oz.)	5
Milk chocolate (1 oz.)	6
Dark chocolate, semi-sweet (1 oz.)	20
Baker's chocolate (1 oz.)	26
Chocolate-flavored syrup (1 oz.)	4

Source: FDA, Food Additive Chemistry Evaluation Branch, based on evaluations of existing literature on caffeine levels.

Soft Drinks (12-oz. serving)	
Sugar-Free Mr. PIBB	58.8
Mountain Dew	54.0
Mello Yello	52.8
TAB	46.8
Coca-Cola	45.6
Diet Coke	45.6
Shasta Cola	44.4
Shasta Cherry Cola	44.4
Shasta Diet Cola	44.4
Mr. PIBB	40.8

Dr. Pepper	39.6
Sugar-Free Dr. Pepper	39.6
Big Red	38.4
Sugar-Free Big Red	38.4
Pepsi-Cola	38.4
Aspen	36.0
Diet Pepsi	36.0
Pepsi Light	36.0
RC Cola	36.0
Diet Rite	36.0
Kick	31.2
Canada Dry Jamaica Cola	30.0
Canada Dry Diet Cola	1.2

Source: Institute of Food Technologists (IFT), April 1983, based on data from National Soft Drink Association, Washington, D.C. IFT also reports that there are at least 68 flavors and varieties of soft drinks produced by 12 leading bottlers that have no caffeine.

Prescription Drugs	Milligrams of caffeine
Cafergot (for migraine headaches)	100
Fiorinal (for tension headaches)	40
Soma Compound (muscle relaxant)	32
Darvon Compound (pain relief)	32.4

Nonprescription Drugs

Weight-Control Aids	
Dex-A-Diet II	200
Dexatrim Extra Strength	200
Dietac capsules	200
Maximum Strength Appedrine	100
Prolamine	140

Alertness Tablets	
Nodoz	100
Vivarin	200
Analgesic/Pain Relief	
Anacin, Maximum Strength Anacin	32
Excedrin	65
Midol	32.4
Vanquish	33
Diuretics	
Aqua-Ban	100
Maximum Strength Aqua-Ban Plus	200
Permathene H2 Off	200
Cold/Allergy Remedies	
Coryban-D capsules	30
Triaminicin tablets	30
Dristan Decongestant tablets,	
Dristan A-F Decongestant tablets	16.2
Duradyne-Forte	30

Source: FDA's National Center for Drugs and Biologics. FDA also notes that caffeine is an ingredient in more than 1,000 nonprescription drug products as well as numerous prescription drugs.

Considering all the forms caffeine comes in, it's easy to see how you can go way over the acceptable limit of 200 mg per day. If you drink two cups of coffee plus a can of soda and take a couple of cold tablets containing caffeine, you've consumed 335 mg. Add a couple of Excedrin and it jumps to 465 mg. One more cup of coffee tops out at 580 mg. It's very easy for your caffeine consumption to escalate far above the healthy level (see Figure 5.2).

In some ways caffeine seems like the perfect answer when you're looking for extra energy. Coffee, for example, is a socially acceptable, addictive drink that keeps you alert and awake with almost no calories (around 5 calories per cup of black coffee).[22] But you pay a price for the energy you get from caffeine.

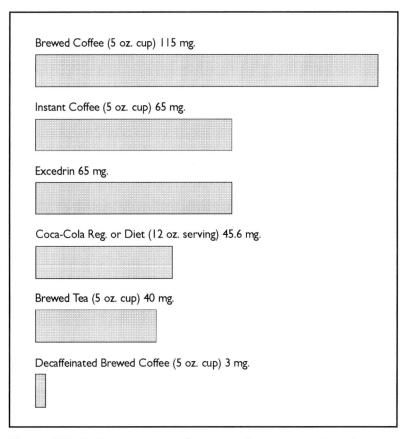

Figure 5.2 Caffeine content of common beverages and medication.

Caffeine artificially stimulates the central nervous system. Beginning with the brain, it has a direct effect on the part of the brain that controls heart rate and respiration. It accelerates both of these functions. Caffeine restricts the blood vessels going to the brain and dilates those going to the heart and lungs. Caffeine relaxes the muscles of the digestive tract including the kidneys. The kidneys increase urinary output causing caffeine to have a diuretic effect.[23]

Perhaps most importantly, caffeine stimulates the adrenal glands to secrete adrenaline. This triggers the entire stress response called the flight or fight response (see Chapter 3).

Your body essentially doesn't know the difference between a man with a gun and a cup of coffee. In both situations the body reacts by pumping out a rush of adrenaline.

Dr. Dean Ornish points out that "although we sometimes believe that caffeine *gives* us energy, it only *borrows* energy from the future."[24] The surge of adrenaline leaves us feeling even more tired once it has worn off. This, of course, may send us right back to the coffee pot or soda machine to get another hit of caffeine. This cycle of addiction is more acceptable than that of street drugs like cocaine and heroin, but not much different.

Withdrawing from caffeine will let you know exactly how strong the drug is. If you go cold-turkey after drinking a lot of caffeine, you'll experience symptoms much like the flu for several days. You'll suffer from a headache along with body aches and lethargy. (See Healthy Suggestion #4 for ways to deal with caffeine withdrawal.) In fact, some people who suffer from what they think are tension headaches every day, may actually be suffering from caffeine withdrawal on a daily basis. If you get relief from these headaches by taking pain relievers containing caffeine (see chart) or by drinking coffee, that's a clue that you may be suffering from withdrawal. This is especially true if regular aspirin, which doesn't contain caffeine, won't help.[25]

Caffeine comes with a cost that is not worth it for most broadcasters. You are already working in one of the most stress-filled environments, and you don't need to increase that stress chemically. We all know that heavy coffee drinking brings on symptoms like jitteriness, shortness of breath, rapid heart beat (possibly even abnormal heart rhythms), and upset stomach. These are some of the exact symptoms of panic attacks (see Chapter 3). Panic attacks are a real threat when you're working under a lot of stress. Don't increase your likelihood of feeling these symptoms by consuming lots of caffeine.

Sugar

Our bodies were not designed to handle concentrated amounts of refined sugar. When these are consumed in the form of things like candy bars, doughnuts, and sweetened sodas, the body goes into overdrive. Sugar affects the body in much the same way that caffeine does. (Imagine the effect of coffee with sugar in it!)

Let's look at what happens when you can't resist that chocolate doughnut you find lurking in the coffee room. Once you've eaten it, your blood sugar rises rapidly. Your body thinks because of the amount of sugar it gets there will be lots of food coming in with it. As a result, your pancreas pumps out enough insulin to handle the whole load.[26] But not enough food follows. The insulin goes to every cell in the body (except in the brain) and causes them to open and admit the sugar.[27] Insulin sweeps the sugar out of your blood. This happens very rapidly, and your blood sugar level drops (see Figure 5.3). But the pancreas can not stop excreting insulin fast enough so your blood sugar level may drop even lower than it was when you first bit into the doughnut.[28]

A concentrated sugar dose that comes without much other food will cause this reaction in your body. Cane sugar, brown sugar, raw sugar, honey, and concentrated fruit juice all have the same effect on the blood sugar level.

Most of us know when we bite into a doughnut we're eating sugar, but sugar hides in many foods. Many breakfast cereals have sugar listed as the first or second ingredient which means it is the primary ingredient. 100 percent fruit juices vary widely in their amount of sugar. One small box of cranberry/raspberry drink, for example, may have as many as 38 grams of sugar. Four grams of sugar are equal to one teaspoon of table sugar so this boxed drink would give you over nine teaspoons of sugar. That's more than the doughnut. Check food labels for the grams of sugar which

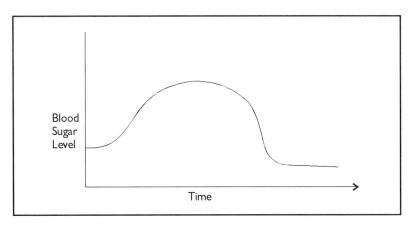

Figure 5.3 Eating refined or simple sugar may cause your blood sugar level to drop even lower than it was before you consumed the sugar. (Adapted from *Dr. Dean Ornish's Program for Reversing Heart Disease.*)

may be listed as fructose, high-fructose corn syrup, sucrose, corn sweetener, corn syrup, honey, or glucose dextrose.

Here are some other places extra sugar may sneak into your diet:[29]

Sugar Content

Cake, frosted	1 slice	6 added teaspoons
Low-fat yogurt w/fruit	1 cup	7 added teaspoons
Chocolate shake	10 fl. oz.	9 added teaspoons
Cola	12 fl.oz.	9 added teaspoons
Fruit drink, ade	12 fl. oz.	12 added teaspoons

There is no physiological need for refined sugar in our nutritional requirements. Sugar gives us empty calories and has a severe effect on our blood sugar levels. But that doesn't stop most of us from grabbing it when we feel our energy dropping. A client who works in a television bureau where the deadline pressures are especially intense told me this story. Every day at deadline time, the clerk from the coffee shop in the building comes through the newsroom selling candy bars. They nicknamed him "Chocolate Bob," and my client said when she looks up from her computer, it's as if he has a halo over his head. He can overcharge for the candy. No one cares. They just need that sugar fix. And when he doesn't show up for some reason, everyone suffers.

How can you break this sugar craving? Just like with caffeine, you must cut down slowly. Don't go cold-turkey. Eat a couple of chocolate kisses instead of a whole candy bar. Split the doughnut and order a kiddie cone instead of two scoops. It's not necessary or fun to deprive yourself of all the treats you love. Just make small changes, and they will begin to reduce your desire to have excess sugar in your diet.

Alcohol

Drinking alcohol increases your sugar intake. Like refined sugar, alcohol gives you only empty calories. Unlike sugar and caffeine, it has an anesthetic effect on the body. It works as a depressant putting the brain to sleep, starting with the frontal lobe, or reasoning portion, of the brain. Alcohol also has a diuretic effect causing the body to lose fluid (see Water section that follows).

Alcohol is actually toxic to the body, affecting the brain, heart, liver, and gastrointestinal tract.[30] There's controversy in the medical field about whether moderate intake (no more than two drinks a day) may be beneficial. Some studies have shown that even moderate intake of alcohol may double your risk of stroke and increase a woman's risk of breast cancer. Considering this and the fact that somewhere between 50 and 80 percent of the nation's traffic deaths involve alcohol, it should be used with caution.[31]

If you drink to relax, be especially careful how much you rely on alcohol. One network television producer told me at first she really needed a glass of wine when she came home to unwind. Later that became two glasses, and finally she found she was drinking most of a bottle every night. This is when she realized she had a problem. If you begin to depend on "Happy Hour," think about other ways to relax. The relaxation suggestions in Chapter 6 and exercise as described in Chapter 4 are much healthier ways to relieve stress after a tough day.

Salt

We can get all the sodium our bodies need for an entire day (around 2400 milligrams) without ever adding salt to anything.[32] Look at these sources of sodium in our diet:

Sodium Content

	Amount of Food	Amount of sodium
Ham, lean	3 ounces	1020 milligrams
Dill pickle	1 medium	930 milligrams
Corn chips	1 ounce	235 milligrams
Bread	1 slice	175 milligrams
Tomato Juice, canned	3/4 cup	660 milligrams
Vegetable soup	1 cup	820 milligrams
Process cheeses	2 ounces	800 milligrams
Soy sauce	1 tablespoon	1030 milligrams
Coca Cola	12 ounces	50 milligrams

As you can see, it's not hard to get the 2400 mg of sodium we need in our diet without adding any extra.

Salt makes us thirsty. When we do get more salt in our bodies than we need, we crave extra water to dilute it. This is important because the body maintains a precise concentration of salt, and we must bring in enough water to keep this ratio within a narrow range. The negative effect of this is that with too much salt we retain the water which increases our weight and may have an effect on blood pressure. Therefore, it's important to go easy on salt and foods that are high in sodium like cured meats, luncheon meats, most cheeses, canned soups and vegetables, and soy sauce.[33]

Water

Caffeine, sugar, and salt are all foods to limit because of their effects on the body, but water is one thing we can increase. Water is the single most important nutrient in our bodies. In fact, almost two-thirds of our body weight is water. It's almost as if water invented the human body so it could transport itself from place to place.[34]

Every one of our bodily functions occurs in the medium of water.[35] Water regulates our body temperature, plays a vital role in digestion and waste removal, cleanses our blood, carries nutrients and oxygen to our cells, cushions our joints, and helps nerve impulse connection. Our brain is seventy-five percent fluid. We have an internal sea in our bodies that we can't live without.[36]

But the sad fact is that most of us pay more attention to watering our lawns and house plants than we do our bodies. This is despite the fact that we are constantly losing water. We routinely lose ten cups a day by sweating, breathing, and eliminating wastes from our bodies.[37] And during strenuous exercise we may lose two quarts of water (eight cups) in an hour from sweating alone.[38] This water loss can be significant. Even a small amount of dehydration (around one percent of body weight) can affect our physiological state and our performance.[39]

The first place the body goes for water if dehydration begins is to the blood. With less blood volume, there is less fluid to pump, and our internal organs have to work harder.[40] Reduced blood volume also means less oxygen and nutrients for the muscles and other organs. Our digestion becomes less efficient, and we may begin to retain water to make up for the dehydration.[41]

With all these negative things occurring, why is it so hard to drink enough water to stay hydrated? One reason is that our thirst mechanism is not set appropriately. This may be because our ancestors had trouble finding fresh water so it's set to keep them from being constantly thirsty. But for us, it makes getting the water we need even harder.

Our thirst signal shuts off at about 68 percent of hydration when we're drinking water. That means that if we drink water until we don't feel thirsty anymore, we will still be 32 percent dehydrated. One reason sports drinks work for hydration is that they contain sodium which makes us thirsty. But even with a sports drink, our thirst signal still shuts off at 82 percent of hydration.[42] To get the water we need in our bodies, we can't depend on whether we're thirsty or not. We have to literally force fluids all day long.

Water stays in our stomachs about fifteen minutes. For it to help hydrate our tissues, we have to process it through our stomachs so that it can get into our organs and tissue. Looking at the vocal folds as an example, moisture works to cushion the folds as they open and close for speech. It works much like oil in a car to protect this delicate tissue. Gargling and swallowing water doesn't get it down into the throat far enough to reach the vocal folds. We have to take the water in systemically so that it keeps the folds plump and moist and maintains the correct viscosity of the mucous in the throat. This means ingesting water throughout the day.

Many people ask me why it has to be water. It doesn't have to be, but it must be decaffeinated, unsweetened, non-alcoholic fluid. Other choices include low-fat milk which is 90 percent water, or yogurt which is mostly water, herbal teas, decaffeinated coffee or tea, fruit juices (preferably 100 percent juice diluted 50/50 with water), and fruits which are about 90 percent water. Some of these have drawbacks, however. Dairy products make a condition in the throat that may produce excessive mucus which is a problem if you're on-air. And it's hard to measure how much water is in fruit and yogurt. Flavored waters also can be a good choice if they do not contain sugar. Seltzer water and club soda may contain sodium so check the label before consuming large quantities of either.

Looking at the choices, just plain water seems the best. Drink it cool (around 40-50 degrees) for the quickest absorption. Warm and ice water move into our systems slower.[43] You can flavor water with a twist of lemon or lime or drink sparkling water if you find it too hard to drink plain. But water is cheap and readily available so there are few excuses for not drinking it. You can purchase bottled water if you find the chlorine taste too strong in your tap water or if you live in a city with poor drinking water (see Healthy Suggestion #5 to find out if your water is safe). A water purifier will help improve the taste of tap water. You can have a filter installed in your home or newsroom, or you can purchase your own from one of the companies like Brita. A pitcher with a filtering device can be helpful for the newsroom if you often forget to buy bottled water.

Calculating how much water to drink is simple if you use the ratio devised by the International SportsMedicine Institute. They work with Olympic athletes and have done research on how much water we need. Their formula has been used for over two decades. A non-active person (one who doesn't exercise), needs one-half ounce of water per pound of body weight per day. If you exercise regularly, you need two-thirds ounce per pound of body weight.[44] You should seek expert advice on water intake if you do strenuous, endurance exercise for long periods of time such as marathon running.

If you don't work out, for example, and you weigh 140 pounds, you will need to drink 70 ounces of water a day (or get the equivalent from other sources given above). A tall bottle of water like Evian is around 50 ounces. That means to get the 70 ounces, you need one tall bottle and about half of another one. Filling one tall bottle each day and making certain you drink at least that much can be a good start. Replace your coffee cup at work with a plastic stadium cup or a sports bottle, and drink from it all day long.

Your reaction at this point may be like most of my clients: Good grief, I'll spend all day in the bathroom! Broadcasters working outside in the field see this as a big problem. And it may be true that during the first week you'll notice a difference, but your body will quickly adapt to the increase of water. And you'll see and feel the benefits very quickly. Staying more hydrated will help your voice, your energy level, your digestion, your skin, and almost every one of your internal organs.

I'm often asked another question: Isn't it possible to drink too much water? Actually, unless you have an extremely rare psychiatric disorder called psychogenic polydipsia, a compulsion to drink water, you will not get too much.[45] It may feel like a lot to you, but that's just because you may have been dehydrated most of your life. Because caffeine and alcohol are diuretics, it is especially important to increase your water intake when you consume these drugs. When you're drinking alcohol, replace your water ounce for ounce. To stay hydrated, for every glass of alcohol you drink, take in a glass of water. Caffeine is not quite as bad as alcohol, but it prevents your body from retaining 100 percent of the fluid you consume.[46] Don't depend on either alcohol or caffeinated fluids to reach your appropriate fluid intake each day.

Here is a checklist you can use to review your daily food and water needs:

Daily Nutritional Checklist

1. Combine **1/3 protein, 2/3 carbohydrates**, and a **small amount of fat** in every meal and snack.

2. Eat a variety of foods.

3. Eat a meal or snack **every four hours.**

4. Always eat a breakfast that contains protein, carbohydrates, and a small amount of fat.

5. Limit your intake of caffeine, sugar, alcohol, and salt.

6. Drink at least **half your body weight in ounces of water daily.**

7. Don't eat a heavy meal two hours before sleeping.

Healthy Suggestions

1 Make a list of what you have eaten and drunk so far today. Add the rest of what you eat to that at the end of the day and review it. How much did you eat? When did you eat? Where did you eat? Did you drink enough water? Did you eat a variety of foods? Did you drink much alcohol? How much? Caffeine? How much? Sugar? How much? Salt? How much? Analyze your diet for the day. If you find it lacking, do this exercise again tomorrow, and try to improve.

2 Grazing, or eating five small meals a day, can be a good way to keep your blood sugar up and get a variety of foods. Try combining your grazing meals with relaxation. Take at least five minutes and eat while you do something to relax like walking around the building or looking out the window. If you must eat at your desk, try listening to some pleasant music while wearing a headset so that you take a break from the newsroom while you eat. Better yet, go outside or into a quiet conference room to eat. The less stressed we are when we eat, the better our digestion will be.

3 If you diet quite a bit or have trouble remembering to eat, take this quiz adapted from Dr. Christine Northrup's book, *Women's Bodies, Women's Wisdom:*

Do You Have a 'Diet Mentality'?

- Are you so afraid of gaining weight that you routinely avoid food you really love?

- Do you avoid eating all day so that you can binge at night?

- At a buffet, do you routinely tell yourself you can't have what you really want?

- Do you allow yourself to get so hungry that you gulp whatever is available, rarely tasting it?

- Do you routinely drink coffee or caffeinated diet drinks during the day as a substitute for food?

- If you gain a pound does it ruin your day and affect what you eat?

A "yes" answer to any of these may mean you are more focused on staying thin instead of staying healthy.[47]

4 If you are now consuming more caffeine than you want, set realistic goals for yourself to change that. Going cold-turkey will make you feel awful, and may make you more prone to give in and return to caffeine. Here are some ideas for cutting back:

- Week 1: Slowly cut back your caffeine by half. You can drink the same amount of coffee or soda, but make half of it decaf. If you think decaf coffee tastes different (which is not true since caffeine is taste-less), you can mix decaf and regular together.

- Week 2: Cut back one-half again on caffeine and increase your water intake.

- Week 3: Eliminate all caffeine and reach one-half your body weight in ounces of water.

5 If you want to find out if your water is safe to drink, call the Environmental Protection Agency's Safe

Drinking Water Hotline at 800-426-4791. Information about bottled water is available from the International Bottled Water Association at 800-WATER 11.

6 Replacing fluids when you're exercising is especially important. Covert Bailey, one of the country's foremost health and fitness experts, makes the following recommendations in his book, *Smart Exercise:*

1. Drink a cup of water a half hour before exercising.

2. Drink three to six ounces of fluid every 15 or 20 minutes during exercise.

3. Don't wait to be thirsty. You will get dehydrated if you wait until you notice your thirst.

4. Drink cool fluids. Fluids at 40 to 50 degrees pass through the stomach and into the bloodstream more quickly than warm or iced fluids.

5. After exercise, fruit juices or sports drinks are better for rehydration, but they are not really needed unless you exercise hard for more than one hour.[48]

7 If you want to get some help designing an eating program that works best for you, you can call the American Dietetic Association at 800-366-1655 to get a referral for a registered dietitian in your area. Anyone can call oneself a nutritionist. If you decide to work with someone, make certain they have a legitimate diploma as a registered dietitian (R.D.) or an M.S. or Ph.D. in nutrition studies.

8 You can figure the number of grams of fat that provide 30 percent of calories in your daily diet as follows: Multiply your total day's calories by 0.30 to get your calories from fat per day. Example: 2,200 calories × 0.30 = 660 calories from fat. Next divide the calories from fat per day by 9 (each gram of fat has 9 calories) to get grams of fat per day. If you eat 2,200 calories you should have 73 grams of fat per day.

6
Learning To Relax

From the Newsroom:
Chris McKendry, Anchor/Reporter
SportsCenter, ESPN

I never feel the actual job is stressful for me because I love it so much, and it's what I'm trained to do. I don't stress out when I have to sit down and anchor for an extra hour, or if we have to fill time because the show is expanded following a game. But what I find stressful are the surrounding, little things that come with being on-air. When I worked for a Washington, D.C., affiliate, it was very stressful. The demands on you once you left work were amazing. Some weeks it was four appearances a week. It was like a second job. Being a sportscaster was my first job and being Chris McKendry was my second job. It's really stressful when all of a sudden you have no time for yourself. A woman I work with said, "You know what stresses me out? When it comes time to write the bills. Where's the time to do it?" Those little things like taking your car in and remembering birthdays. Sometimes it's the wacky time schedules, too. You don't always have that Saturday when you get your errands done. It's never the big things, it is always that final little thing that can send you into stress orbit. Our show is an hour which is a big change from being a sportscaster that gets three minutes. To relax from that I do things that take my mind onto something totally different like playing golf. It's great because you go out on the course, and you get totally lost in it. That helps a lot. Even if you're tired from work when you do something where you're not thinking about the work, suddenly you're not tired. Go to a different arena, and get your mind off work. It makes you better at your job. That's what I think I'm finally realizing. Doing other things and finding other interests, makes you better. I'm very lucky because I can go to make-up. It might be just 15 minutes, but in those 15 minutes nobody's allowed to come get me. It's being away from the whole newsroom and everybody saying, What's going on with this page? Did you hear the latest on that? That 15 minutes can really help. I also use my breathing exercises to relax. And I always take a few real deep breaths just to remind myself to breathe deeply. When I'm excited or stressed, I tend to breathe shallowly. I have to be very focused and for that hour I can't even think about everything else that is going on. If I'm nervous, I can't explain to the world that I've had a really bad day. They don't care. I say to myself, "You can do this. You are going to do this. You know how to do this."

Learning To Relax

There is more to life than increasing its speed.
Gandhi

The poet, Richard Eberhart, sums up the lives of many broadcasters when he writes, "If I could only live at the pitch that is near madness."[1] I think of this line often when I witness the pressures of working in broadcasting. As you know, it is a world of deadlines, crises, noise, confusion, and pressure. A newsroom is not a place that's conducive to relaxation. In fact, you may think it's a joke even to consider the idea of adding any relaxation to your hectic life. When I suggested to one client that she take two weeks off from her job as a radio reporter so she could relax, she said I might as well ask her to fly to the moon. For her, it wasn't even a consideration.

As you've already read, taking care of yourself as a broadcaster is no luxury. It's a necessity. You should stay in shape because stress can sabotage your performance and wreck your health. To take good care of yourself, you need the daily preventive medicine of relaxation. This doesn't mean joining a meditation group or going off to a retreat center somewhere. Being able to relax is an ability we all have, and we can do it anywhere. Most of us move farther and farther away from it, but we can always regain the ability to relax. As one television ad puts it, if you take some letters out of the word, "calamity," you can get, "calm."

What Is Relaxation?

Relaxing is not a sophisticated art form that takes months to learn. The bottom line of relaxation is that you have to let your mind go from point A to point B. In point B you wipe the slate clean of stress so when you return to point A, you are relaxed. Point A might be the daily stress of getting a show ready if you're a producer or the crunch of meeting a deadline with your story if you're a reporter. These are stressful events. Point B would be a place that allows you to forget about the stressful event for a few minutes. It's that feeling of being "a million miles away" in your mind. This can be accomplished by any of the ways presented in this chapter. It is not important which one you choose. If one doesn't work for you, simply try another one. You might focus on your breathing for a few minutes, for example, or do some visualization. Whatever you choose, the relaxation will give your body and mind a break.

Relaxation breaks are important to include throughout your day. No magic technique or pill will instantly erase a build-up of stress. If you think of each stressful event as a stair step, you cannot go down a whole flight in one giant step (see Figure 6.1). You can't yell, "Relax!," at yourself and expect results. But if you have taken relaxation breaks throughout your day, you can keep yourself from building that stairway of stress. You will be experiencing the normal stress cycle that you read about in Chapter 3 (see Figure 3.1). You will be coming down from the stress before it becomes unmanageable.

Jon Kabat-Zinn, who heads up the Stress Reduction Clinic at the University of Massachusetts Medical Center, explains relaxation best when he says that the basic idea of any form of relaxation is to "create an island of *being* in the sea of constant *doing* in which our lives are usually immersed."[2] Relaxation allows us to slow down our minds and bodies in order to take a break from the hectic world in which we live

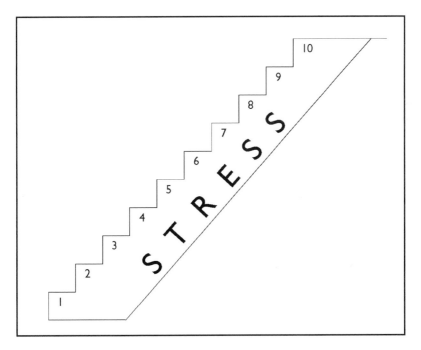

Figure 6.1 You cannot come down the stairsteps of stress in one giant leap. Stress reduction must happen on step 1 or 2, not step 10.

and work. It doesn't require hours to do this. A few relaxation breaks throughout the day can reap big results.

Other countries honor times to relax more than we do. It's common practice in most European countries to close offices and shops for two hours in the middle of the day for a break. In our offices it's more common to see someone with a sandwich in one hand and a phone in the other. When I work in newsrooms and corporate buildings, I am constantly amazed by how little time people give themselves to relax even when they eat. I'm usually the only one having lunch on the patio or deck that's provided for staff. Everyone else is eating at their desks (or not eating at all). But something as simple as watching the birds and looking at the sky for a few minutes can be a great relaxer. When you return to your work, you'll be refreshed which will make you more productive.

If you remember the last time you were recovering from an illness, you may remember the delight of something as mundane as sitting outside. You may have been able to rediscover the simplest pleasures like the sun on your face, and your thoughts may have been totally focused in the present. The same thing usually happens with a vacation. Feeling the sand between your toes on a beach or listening to the crunch of snow if you're skiing, brings a special delight. And when you return from vacation, the things that you love about your job become apparent instead of the stressors that drive you crazy. You move at a different rhythm for a while.

But you can't wait fifty weeks for those two weeks of vacation and expect it to reduce your stress all year long. Relaxation needs to be a daily destination. It's a little like sewing a parachute. You don't wait until the plane is going down to begin sewing. You work on the parachute every day so it will be ready in an emergency.[3] If you practice relaxation daily, you'll be able to respond to crisis situations with a new sense of calm.

This is especially true in the fast-paced world in which we live. All the technological devices that are supposed to save us time like fax machines, cellular phones, and the internet, have simply made us more accessible. As a broadcaster, you're now available any time of the day or night, anywhere in the world. There may seem to be no way to escape. As a by-product of this, your mind and nervous system may stay in an overstimulated state. When a pager goes off, we all jump. Our bodies and minds may act like muscles that are always flexed.

And we often eliminate the pleasurable things from our lives when we need them the most. One client recently told me he had changed dry cleaners even though he loved to chat with the owner of his old cleaners when he took his clothes in. He felt that because his old cleaners was ten minutes out of his way, he should pick one that was on his route home. The pressures of his life had caused him to abandon one of the few relaxing moments he had every week.

Taking Time to Relax

Clients have shared with me many ways they relax in the stressful world of broadcasting. One told me that he loves to get stuck in a traffic jam because he turns off his phone and his radio and relaxes. He feels he can't go anywhere and no one can reach him so he might as well take a relaxation break. Another client said she does the same thing when she first gets home. She keeps the house quiet and just sits and breathes for a few minutes in the silence. One radio anchor said she retreats to the restroom several times a day to get out of the hectic newsroom. She spends a few minutes there concentrating on her breathing. A reporter told me she carries a small book of poetry with her and reads it when she's out in the field waiting to cover an event. This takes her away from the scene around her, and when she needs to go to work, she's less stressed. There are unlimited ways to bring a few moments of relaxation into your life (see Healthy Suggestions).

Most of us know how good it feels to relax. We also know that relaxation helps us cope, but it still may be hard to take the time. Many people tell me they feel guilty when they relax. They feel lazy. And it's usually the people who need to relax the most who are the ones who fight it the hardest. They do not realize that many times when you push the hardest, you get the least results. This is certainly true of broadcast delivery. Relaxation is the key to good delivery, not the extra effort that comes when you push harder. A little relaxation will improve any voice.

One example of this came from an anchor I was working with who suddenly had her duties tripled when two other anchors had to take sick leave. She went from anchoring the evening news to anchoring two news shows plus a daily talk show. This was to be for only a week, so her idea was to push as hard as she could to make it through the week and then relax. I pointed out to her that if she adjusted her life outside of work during that week, she could improve her stress level and her performance as well. I suggested she throw everything that wasn't imperative overboard and replace those activities with things that were relaxing. Instead of doing the laundry that week, for example, I advised her to use that hour to have a massage. I suggested she have meals delivered so she could soak in a hot tub instead of spending time in a hot kitchen. Activities like these would care for and honor her while giving her some needed relaxation. These changes could help make a difficult week one that could be tolerable, and she would not find herself exhausted at the end of the week.

Since it's a guarantee that the stresses of working in broadcasting will not go away, it's important to look at ways to take control of how you deal with the stresses. There are really three components to a stressful situation: 1) the event that triggers the problem, 2) the way you perceive it, and 3) the coping skills you have to help you deal with the stress. You have little control over the first component. The second one may take some time to change, but the third one is within your immediate control. Coping skills can be learned.

The Relaxation Response

In 1975, Dr. Herbert Benson, a professor at Harvard Medical School and director of the hypertension section of

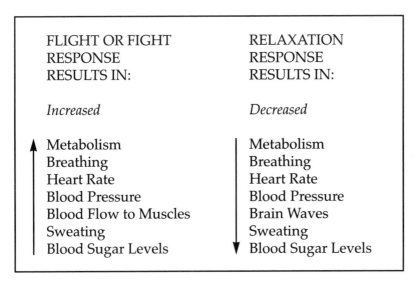

FLIGHT OR FIGHT RESPONSE RESULTS IN:	RELAXATION RESPONSE RESULTS IN:
Increased	*Decreased*
Metabolism	Metabolism
Breathing	Breathing
Heart Rate	Heart Rate
Blood Pressure	Blood Pressure
Blood Flow to Muscles	Brain Waves
Sweating	Sweating
Blood Sugar Levels	Blood Sugar Levels

Figure 6.2 The benefits of the Relaxation Response.

Boston's Beth Israel Hospital, published a book called *The Relaxation Response.* This response is the opposite of the flight or fight response (see Figure 6.2). It can be elicited by using many different relaxation techniques like you'll read about in this chapter. The goal of each of these is to reach the relaxed state which Dr. Benson calls the Relaxation Response. Dr. Benson believes this can relieve the stress that leads to high blood pressure, hardening of the arteries, heart attack, and stroke. He says it will also lessen fatigue, help a person cope with anxiety, improve sleep, and increase alertness. At the time the book came out, these must have seemed like outrageous promises. Now researchers around the world have proven repeatedly that what Dr. Benson proposed is true. As one recent book puts it, "The Relaxation Response is to stress-related illness what aspirin is to everyday aches and pains — a reliable source of relief."[4]

Scientific studies of the Relaxation Response prove its effectiveness. One study showed that volunteers who listened to relaxation tapes or practiced relaxation techniques got an immediate increase in the substance (interleukin-1) that is an essential link in the chain reactions that fight off disease.[5]

The Relaxation Response is also standard therapy for anxiety. Learning to incorporate relaxation into your daily life has been shown to help prevent a stress build-up that can result in a panic attack. Doing some relaxation every day is like putting out brush fires before they build into a fire storm. The fire storms of stress are panic attacks as well as other life-threatening health problems.

In addition to helping build immunity and lessen anxiety, relaxation has also been shown to have a positive effect on blood pressure and many heart related illnesses. Research in this area has been done by many scientists including Dr. Dean Ornish, who includes relaxation as part of his plan to reverse heart disease.

In Chapter 3 you read about what happens to our bodies when we become stressed. Stress causes our heart rate and blood pressure to rise, we breathe more rapidly, blood leaves our extremities and goes to our large muscles and our body generally goes on alert (see Figure 6.2). This is an automatic response that occurs in a matter of seconds.

The Relaxation Response is not automatic. It takes practice to learn and discipline to incorporate into daily life, but when we achieve the Relaxation Response our heart rates and blood pressures drop, our breathing slows, blood flows into our hands and feet and warms them, and our brain waves switch from being very active (beta-rhythm) to being calm (alpha-rhythm). The calm brain waves approximate the vibration of the earth which may be one reason why the Relaxation Response is so effective.[6] It is in effect a "counterbalancing mechanism"[7] to the flight or fight response that causes so much distress in our bodies. In fact, twenty minutes of deep relaxation can rest and revive both the mind and the body as much as two hours of sleep.[8]

So if relaxation is so effective, why isn't everyone doing it every day? That may be because it is a learned skill. It's like lifting weights. You have to begin slowly and work on it over many sessions to feel improvement. We may not feel like we're getting anything from relaxation periods because we can't see what's happening inside our bodies. But while we're relaxing, certain parts of our brains are being stimulated in a different way. Physiological changes are happening. What feels like doing nothing is actually very productive. Relaxing is preventing stress-related problems. We may be doing what Nobel Peace Prize nominee, Thich Nhat Hanh, suggests: "Taking a break, to avoid a breakdown."[9]

Ways to Reach the Relaxation Response

Now that you know the positive effects of relaxing, let's look at ways to achieve the Relaxation Response. Remember that the basic idea is to do something that will allow your mind to move from the thoughts it is dealing with to another place. Then when you return to your previous thoughts, you will be refreshed. There are many ways to do this, but we will be looking at five basic relaxation techniques: breathing, focused relaxation, visualization, affirmations, and assisted techniques like biofeedback and massage.

Breathing

The simple act of breathing is the biggest ally of relaxation. Conscious breathing is something we can turn to in an instant to slow down our minds and bodies. It's always available to us. Breathing has been used for thousands of years for this exact purpose. In the ancient philosophy of yoga, for example, the breath is called prana and is considered the life force. In this philosophy it is believed that if you can control the breath you can control the mind. Understanding breathing and using it to assist you with relaxation is the first step in beginning to control your stress level.

Each day we take between 15,000 and 20,000 breaths, bringing in oxygen-rich air and exhaling carbon dioxide. Most of these breaths are controlled by our sympathetic nervous system which means they happen automatically as a life-support function. We don't have to think about breathing. This is fortunate since when we're sleeping we want to continue breathing. But our breathing can also be controlled by the parasympathetic part of our nervous system, which means we can take control of it. Like blinking or swallowing, we can do it consciously or we can forget about it and let it function by itself.

When we inhale, we create a vacuum in our chests by expanding the rib cage. The earth's atmosphere will not tolerate a vacuum if there is a way for air to enter. When there's a vacuum in our chests, the atmospheric pressure pushes air into that space, and we automatically inhale a breath. To expand our chests and create a vacuum, we use the muscles surrounding our thoracic or chest cavity (see Figure 6.3).

One way we can expand our chests is by hoisting the shoulders up to make the top of the thoracic cavity expand. This is called upper chest or clavicular breathing. This is not the recommended manner for breathing because it puts extra tension in the throat area. The vocal folds (cords) are muscles and ligaments that extend out into the throat to create a valve. This valve both protects the lungs from foreign matter and allows us to make sound waves by blowing air through the closed folds.

Tension in the upper chest can move into the throat and affect the pitch of a person's voice by increasing tension in

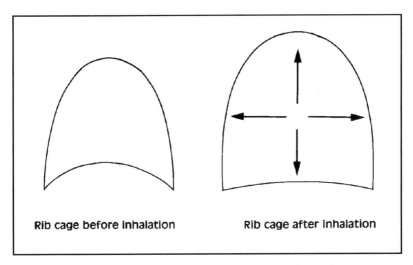

Rib cage before inhalation   Rib cage after inhalation

Figure 6.3 Increase of volume within thorax with inhalation.

the vocal folds. If you want to feel this, take a deep breath right now and force your shoulders up as you inhale. Don't breathe out right away. Can you feel the tightness in your throat? That's what you want to avoid.

Another reason to avoid upper chest breathing if you're an on-air broadcaster is that it will make you more prone to have audible intakes of air on your inhalations. When air is impeded by something, it causes the air to break up into sound waves. If you blow air out through lightly pursed lips, for example, you hear very little. But if you blow over a piece of paper you hear sound. When there's tension in the upper chest you are more likely to feel the need to suck air into your body like a vacuum cleaner. When you do this, your tongue may be slightly raised or your vocal folds may not be completely open. Because of this, you will get an audible intake of air.

You can also inhale by expanding the mid-chest area. This has something in common with the upper chest in-halation in that it uses rather weak muscles to expand the thoracic cavity. This type of breathing will not provide much support for speech because it is rather shallow.

Unfortunately, most of us breathe this way a good bit of the time. It's what I call "socialized breathing" because it allows us to hold our stomachs flat and expand our chests. Whether we're male or female, a flat stomach and a large chest are often the goal. But having this tension in the stomach area forces a type of breathing that is not efficient.

Proper breathing for good speech and relaxation should focus on the use of the diaphragm and the abdominal muscles. The diaphragm is a large, sheet-like muscle that is our primary muscle for breathing. This muscle attaches at the breast bone, under the rib cage, and to the spine. It completely bisects the body with the heart and lungs above the diaphragm in the thoracic cavity and the other organs below in the abdominal cavity. The diaphragm forms a complete floor for the thoracic cavity (see Figure 6.4).

The lungs are spongy masses of tissue with no muscles in them. They rest on the diaphragm which works like a bellows to expand the rib cage for an inhalation. In its resting state, the diaphragm is in a dome-shaped position (see Figure 6.3). On inhalation, the diaphragm muscle contracts downward and flattens out allowing the ribs to flex upward. This movement allows the greatest expansion of the rib cage with the best control. For exhalation, the abdominal muscles control the return of the diaphragm to its resting position just as our arm muscles would control the air going out of a bellows.

When the diaphragm contracts and flattens out, it pushes against the organs below it. This causes the abdomen to expand. This expansion provides an easy way to check your abdominal-diaphragmatic breathing. When you inhale, your stomach should expand, and when you exhale, it should become flatter (see Healthy Suggestion #1).

Relaxed breathing feels like the natural rhythm of waves rising and falling on a beach. When you rest on your back in bed you may feel this rhythm. But during a busy day in the newsroom, this rhythm may be lost. Think of

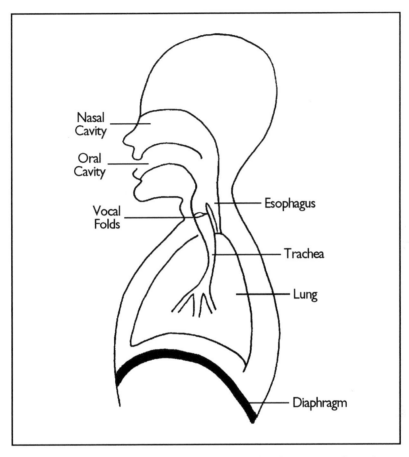

Nasal Cavity

Oral Cavity

Vocal Folds

Esophagus

Trachea

Lung

Diaphragm

Figure 6.4 The main parts of the body involved in proper breathing.

what your body does when you're startled or afraid. You probably hold your breath or breathe shallowly.

Remember how your breathing feels when you're physically active. It speeds up. And when you're anxious, it may really speed up. If you're very anxious you may even hyperventilate which is fast breathing with a loss of the proper breathing rhythm. You eliminate too much carbon dioxide when you hyperventilate. This can result in dizziness and possibly heart palpitations. Hyperventilation can lead to an anxiety attack because the brain does not have what it needs to function properly.

Chapter 3 discusses the physiological effects of the flight or fight response on the body. One effect we get is an armoring of the body. That involves all our muscles but especially the abdominal muscles which can harden during stress. This is a primitive instinct we have to protect our internal organs. But this armoring has a negative effect on our breathing because it prevents the stomach from expanding with each inhalation. It's like wearing a tight girdle all the time that holds in the stomach. Loosening the stomach makes us more vulnerable to attack. When we're stressed, we want to protect ourselves from vulnerability. Stephen Levine offers a wonderful image for changing this in his "soft belly" meditation (see Healthy Suggestion #2). Relaxing the belly allows relaxed breathing and reduces stress.

Our breathing and our emotional states are very closely linked. You may even feel that you tend to synchronize with the events around you and that forces you to react. If the environment is tense, your breathing speeds up or you may hold your breath. If it's relaxed around you, you may be able to breathe slowly and comfortably. But what you will find is that with the use of relaxation techniques you can control your breathing no matter what is going on around you.

Keep in mind that there are two ways that we can breathe. The sympathetic (automatic) nervous system can control our breathing for us, or we can take control with the parasympathetic nervous system. Taking control of your breathing is the first step toward relaxation.

Focused Relaxation

We spend most of our waking hours listening to our racing thoughts. If you could shine a spot light on the part of your body where the majority of your attention is, it would probably be your head most of the time. And that light might look more like a strobe light flashing frantically rather than a solid beam. The Buddhists call this fragmented thinking the "monkey mind" because, like a monkey, it jumps incessantly from thought to thought. Focused relaxation takes us away from the chaos for a short period of time and allows us to be fully present in the moment. It clears the mind much like a glass of muddy water will clear if it is allowed to sit still for a period of time.

The benefits of being able to focus and relax are invaluable for broadcasters. If you're on-air, focus will improve your live shots, your voice, and your performance in general. If you're a writer, producer, or news director, being focused will make you more productive and better able to deal with crises. For all of us, we will be able to ignore distractions and become fully engaged and absorbed in the activities we need to accomplish.

It is impossible to hold two thoughts at the same time. So we can't worry or become anxious when we focus on something positive in the present moment. As Jon Kabat-Zinn explains, "When we can be centered in ourselves, even for brief periods of time in the face of the pull of the outer world . . . we can be at peace with things as they are, moment to moment."[10]

This focus is something we look for in other professionals. Would you want your dentist to seem unfocused and slightly panicked as he begins to work on your teeth? You don't really care that he might have problems in his life at that moment. You want his full attention on you without any distractions. I often advise clients to think of this when they are doing live shots. Even if you are standing in front of a plane that has crashed or a building that has blown up, you need to appear calm and focused. This will help your voice and allow the listener to hear your information without being distracted by your reactions. But as you saw in Figure 6.1, you cannot achieve this in one giant step. You have to build a sense of inner calm over time by learning relaxation techniques.

There are three elements to remember when you begin practicing relaxation. First, you need something to focus your attention on. Working with breathing is an excellent focus to use as you begin your practice because you are very familiar with it. It also works well because it changes your focus from your head to your abdomen. This change of focus alone will give you an instant sense of calm.

The next element to keep in mind is that you want your body to be in a comfortable position. This could be sitting, standing, or lying down, although in a prone position you may be more likely to relax so completely you go to sleep. That may be helpful, too, on occasion, but for daily practice you want to remain awake. You also want to pick a place at least once a day that is fairly quiet. This will allow you to go deeper into your relaxation. But don't limit your relaxing only to quiet places. I encourage you to focus on your breathing in the middle of a busy newsroom or during a crisis to help you relax.

And finally, you want to train yourself to have a passive attitude about your thoughts when you're relaxing. If you're focusing on your breathing, for example, you will have thoughts that come up. It's natural for the mind to wander. This doesn't mean you should stop your relaxation time. Just gently bring your mind back to focusing on your breathing. Try to let other thoughts go.

There may be times when you feel you can't focus your mind at all. But if you keep gently trying, you'll feel more relaxed when you finish. Even if you think all you're doing is sitting and concentrating on your racing thoughts, it's a step in the right direction. The more you try this, the more focused you will be able to become. It isn't necessary for you to go into a deep meditative state to get some benefit from taking a relaxation break.

Many people like to do a little physical exercise prior to relaxing. Some gentle stretching (see Chapter 4) can help, or you might want to burn off energy with some aerobic exercise. In any case, it is best to wake up your mind a little before relaxing. If you've been sitting in the newsroom for several hours, for example, you may become sleepy if you try to relax without moving around first. And if you come home tied in knots from a horribly stressful day, you probably won't have much luck relaxing until you burn off some of the adrenaline left over from the stress. That might be a good time to do a short aerobic workout.

When using breathing to relax, there are many ways you can focus your mind. They will be explained more fully in Healthy Suggestion #3 at the end of this chapter, but the point of all of them is to focus your thoughts on one thing. That might be the feeling of your abdomen expanding when you inhale and contracting when you exhale. It might be focusing on the pauses between the breaths. Or you might feel the temperature changes as the air goes in your nostrils and exits. What you focus on is not important. You simply need to pick something that works for you and stay with it.

Another method of focusing is to pick a word to repeat as you inhale and exhale. You might want to think of the word "relax." You can think "re" as you inhale and "lax" as you exhale. Or you could think of the words "calm" and "peace" as you inhale and exhale. You can also think, "Breathing in," on your inhalation and "Breathing out," on your exhalation. Using words can be helpful since our minds are familiar with them. You can also count your breaths as you relax, thinking one on the first breath, two on the second, etc. Again, what you use is not important.

What's important is that you accomplish the three elements: you are comfortable, your mind is focused on one thing, and you are letting other thoughts pass out of your mind. If you do this for a period of time, you will experience your mind becoming clear. You will be moving from point A which was the stress of your day into point B. You will become focused in the moment. This, as Jon Kabat-Zinn says, "is the direct opposite of taking life for granted."[11] And it is the opposite of being caught up in stress.

Doing relaxation work daily will help you develop a method for dealing with the stress that builds as the day progresses. You will be able to develop cues for yourself that will help you return to a more relaxed place. Once you've done this practice for a while, one deep abdominal-diaphragmatic breath will take you from a stressed place to a relaxed feeling very rapidly. You'll be able to relax throughout your day. You'll no longer have to try to come down that stairway of stress in one giant step (see Figure 6.1). You'll be able to relax as your day progresses.

Breathing is only one way to relax. You may already be thinking of things you do that allow you to reach a relaxed state. I know that if I can spend even ten minutes in the hammock on my deck I will be relaxed. Looking at the trees, the sky, and the birds will definitely take me to point B no matter how stressed my day has been. One client of mine who lives in New York City in a high rise condominium turned her small balcony into a beautiful garden with potted shrubs and flowers. A few minutes tending her garden is all she needs to relax at the end of a hectic day. Another client working in a more rural area bought a horse. She told me that just the thought of going to the stable to be with her horse would relax her in the middle of her workday. Here are some other ideas for relaxing that clients have shared with me:

Running
Skiing
Swimming
Golfing
Walking (see Healthy Suggestion #4)
Doing anything creative like painting, needlework, or
    making pottery
Coloring in a coloring book
Playing with children
Petting an animal
Doing photography for pleasure

Reading a novel
Listening to relaxing music
Taking a long, hot bath or shower
Baking or cooking for pleasure

The one thing all these activities have in common is that they take your mind *off* what's going on in your life. They allow you to become fully absorbed in doing the activity. Spacing out in front of the television or watching a movie may not do that. We often become more stressed during these events depending, of course, on the content. But remember that you want to reach a focused state when relaxing. You want your mind to stop racing and calm down. Most television programs and movies excite rather than calm.

By combining breathing with other ways of having times for focused relaxation, you can structure your day to include lots of relaxation breaks. Here's an example of how you can include relaxation breaks throughout your day:

1. Wake up and focus on breathing for five minutes while still in bed.
2. Driving to work, look at the scenery for part of your commute instead of listening to the radio or talking on the phone.
3. When the phone rings at your desk, take a deep breath before answering it.
4. Walk around outside for a few minutes if you're in the newsroom most of the morning.
5. Eat your lunch while listening to some relaxing music on tape.
6. Take a mid-afternoon break by going to the lunch-room or restroom and concentrating on a word as you inhale and exhale for a few minutes.
7. Before starting your car, sit for a minute and take a deep breath.

8. When you arrive home, sit and concentrate on your breathing in a quiet place for ten or fifteen minutes.
9. Do some gardening or take a walk or read a novel after dinner.
10. When you lie down to go to sleep, concentrate on your breathing until you fall asleep.

This is just one scenario of how your day could include some relaxation breaks. These would take less than an hour from your day. A day is made up of around 960 waking minutes. Taking sixty minutes out of that day to relax is not a big chunk of time. It's your birthright to relax and feel healthy.

There are hundreds of variations of how to design your day so that it includes relaxation. Structure one that personally fits your life and needs. You have the ability to mold your life in this way. These are not big changes, but they can have a profound effect on your stress level. They can allow you to stop your stress throughout the day before it builds to a level that will affect your performance and your health.

Stress begins in the mind. We often think it's driven by outside factors like the people in our lives or the situations we face, but it really begins in our minds. The good thing is that peace begins in our minds as well. We have the ability to control the stress by practicing relaxation.

Visualization

Another relaxation technique that relies on the mind's ability to reduce stress in the body is visualization. This technique has been used by athletes for years. The first sports psychologist was assigned by the U.S. Olympic Committee to teach visualization to our athletes in 1988.[12] Now, 90 percent of Olympic athletes report that they use some form of imagery or visualization to improve their performance.[13]

Visualization is not a complicated skill. It's really nothing more than daydreaming which we all know how to do. But scientific studies have discovered that daydreaming affects the body. For example, visualizing terrible things actually decreases the blood flow to the heart.[14] So when people tell you that your worrying can kill you, they may be correct.

Dreaming at night is another example of the power of visualization. We know that a dream is made up of only mental images, but they can seem so real that they can have a physiological effect on the body. If we're being chased in a nightmare, for example, our pulse rises and we might begin sweating. These physical reactions are observable and can be scientifically measured. Dreaming shows us that our thoughts can produce physical reactions in our bodies.

The same thing occurs when we're awake. If we imagine doing something physical, our muscles respond on a subtle level as if we're doing it. Skiers, for example, were found to have the same muscle response when they imagined racing down a hill as when they actually did it.[15]

The most famous study of visualization was done many years ago at the University of Chicago. People were asked to participate in a study involving throwing a basketball through a hoop. One group came to the gym daily for an hour and practiced free throws. The other group was told to stay home and for an hour each day imagine themselves throwing perfect free throws. At the end of thirty days, the first group showed a 24 percent improvement in throwing the basketball through the hoop. But surprisingly, the group who had never been to the gym to practice and had only used their imaginations, improved at an almost equal level of 23 percent. This proved that for the human nervous system, imagining something in detail is the same as experiencing the real thing.[16]

So how does this apply to broadcasting? Just as an athlete or dancer might imagine an event unfolding perfectly, a broadcaster can do the same thing. This is especially helpful if you're having anxiety about something.

I worked with a television anchor who had experienced a panic attack on air and was terrified that she would have another one. She had reached a level where her anxiety was soaring every night when she sat down at the anchor desk. Her fear and worrying were setting her up emotionally for that to happen. I suggested that ten minutes before going on air she should find a quiet spot and do some visualization. She was to imagine a time when she had done a perfect show. Once she had that feeling, she took herself through the upcoming news hour. She imagined that she was at the top of her game and everything was running smoothly. I had her imagine this in as much detail as possible. By seeing herself as confident and in control, she was able to reduce her anxiety level.

Visualization works because mentally and physically it shows us that a certain outcome is possible. Author Eric Butterworth explains: "Having conceived and deeply felt some thing or experience, you have actually created the condition in the mind that makes a particular outcome inevitable."[17] This is not just wishful thinking, it is scientific fact.

Visualization does not have to be limited to imagining the outcome of an event. It can also be used like a pleasant daydream to take us away from our surroundings for a few minutes. On my desk, for example, are lots of framed photographs taken on vacations I've had in the last few years. I love to gaze at the mountains of Alaska and remember how beautiful it is there. Or I look at a photograph of the waves on the beach in Big Sur and remember how relaxed I felt there. These mini-vacations aren't wasted time. My body is reacting to this relaxation in a physiological way.

Broadcasters have shared with me their ways of using visualization to help them relax. One news director said he redecorated his office when his doctor warned him about his stress level. He realized that all he had on his walls were maps and memos. He replaced those with beautiful paintings of trees and landscapes. Another news director told me she had an aquarium installed in her office. Looking at the fish for a few minutes was all it took for her to relax. This is not surprising because research studies have shown that looking at an aquarium can lower your blood pressure significantly.[18] Clients have also shown me sea shells, plants, photographs, and many other objects that they use to escape for a few minutes into daydreaming. One even told me he relaxes by watching the flow of the graphics on his computer screen saver. There are many ways to use visualization to help you relax.

The experience of visualization is unique for each of us. We all use our senses in different ways when we imagine something. Take a moment right now and imagine you're on a beach. Once you've imagined this, note which senses you're using. Do you see the beach scene like looking at a movie? Do you feel the air on your skin and the sand between your toes? Do you smell the salt air? Get in touch with how your senses work to imagine something. The suggestions in Healthy Suggestion #5 at the end of this chapter will give you more practice with this. You may see the events more than feel or smell them or vice versa. It doesn't matter how you use your senses for visualization, but giving yourself short breaks to visualize can help you deal with stress.

Affirmations

Stress researcher Dr. Hans Selye points out that "Nothing erases unpleasant thoughts more effectively than concentration on pleasant ones."[19] This is the basic principle of using affirmations. Affirmations are positive phrases that you create and repeat over and over to yourself. This is not just a fake, Pollyanna-type attitude. Affirmations actually influence the subconscious and change your view of what's going on in your world.

We are always talking to ourselves. As your day progresses you may say to yourself that this is the most stressful day you've ever had in any newsroom. That may progress to thoughts about how you can't stand your producer which may progress to how you can't tolerate your job. By the end of the day, you may have decided to quit the business altogether. Negative thoughts have a way of multiplying.

I've heard negative or worry thoughts described like this: It's as if you had a bee hive that was empty, and you decided to bring a queen bee from another hive to live in the empty one. One by one the other bees from her hive would come flying over to be with her. Soon the hive would be buzzing with bees. Our thoughts work like this as well. One worry will usually attract others until our head is buzzing with negative thoughts.

A powerful example of this is described by Viktor Frankl in his book, *Man's Search for Meaning*, when relating his experiences in Nazi concentration camps. He explains that the prisoners who gave meaning to their experiences were more likely to survive. He concludes that, "Man *can* preserve a vestige of spiritual freedom, of independence of mind, even in such terrible conditions of psychic and physical stress."[20] The horrors were the same for all prisoners, but the way they thought about their day-to-day experiences affected their survival. It appears that even in hell, there are choices.

No one would compare newsrooms to concentration camps, but they can be negative environments at times. Using affirmations may not change the environment, but they can change how you feel in the environment.

I experienced the benefit of affirmations at the Radio-Television News Directors Association Conference a few years ago. I was assisting with setting up the conference for two days before it began. The first day everything that could go wrong did, and I found myself with an awful headache at the end of the day. I decided I would try using an affirmation to get me through the next day which promised to be worse than the first. I decided that whenever I found myself stressing out I would repeat the phrase, "I am relaxed, and this is fun." I wasn't sure that it would work, but I had nothing to lose. Surprisingly, the affirmation changed my attitude so profoundly that I actually enjoyed the next day despite all the problems that arose. People around me even commented on how my attitude had changed.

To construct an affirmation, look at a negative situation you might have and decide how you'd like it to be different. Then think of a statement that describes the results you want. Always use positive language and make it present tense. In my example, instead of thinking, "This isn't working out, and I feel lousy," I used something positive. If you can't see anything positive, use this list of words to help[21]:

Change this negative ⟶	*To a positive*
can't	can
fear	confident
failure	success
chaos	calm
panic	peace
miserable	happy
depressed	uplifted

Precede these terms with "I am . . ." "I accept . . ." or "I feel. . . ." Create a positive statement and repeat it throughout your day. You might want to give yourself a reminder by placing a written copy of the affirmation on your desk or setting an alarm to go off every hour to make you think of it. Do whatever it takes to remember the affirmation throughout your day.

You can, of course, use quotations from other sources as affirmations. Many people use biblical quotations to keep their attitude positive. One top NASCAR driver, for example, tapes a different biblical quotation to his dashboard before each race. Other people like to use a calendar or daily book of quotations to find their affirmations for the day. Whatever you use should reflect how you want your life to be.

Another way to deal with daily stress through your perception is to use a technique called reframing. This allows you to see events as "interesting" instead of emotionally charged. If, for example, someone speaks to you in an angry way, reframe it. Instead of thinking how awful it was and how much it upset you, replace that thought with the word, "interesting." Instead of thinking, "That was really a 'rude' thing for her to say," replace it with, "That was an 'interesting' thing for her to say." This simple change in thinking gives you more perspective on the event. Your emotions don't get so involved, and you are able to cope with the situation in a more productive way.

You can expand this reframing technique to look at larger situations. This helped one client who was working at her first job in a network newsroom. She said she felt like she was being "sucked into a vortex of negativity" every morning when she came to work. During her first few months there, she found herself becoming more and more depressed. Everyone in the newsroom seemed too hard-driving, stressed, and irritable to her. Reframing helped her shift her perspective to see that her co-workers were really striving for excellence. She was able to change her outlook by reframing events without the negativity so that they became an opportunity for growth as she was challenged to adapt to this environment in healthy ways.

We may not have much control over things that go on around us, but we always have a choice about what we think. We can use affirmations and reframing to replace negative thoughts with positive ones. As John Milton wrote in "Paradise Lost," "The mind is its own place, and in itself can create a Heaven of Hell, a Hell of Heaven."[22] The choice is ours. The responsibility is ours as well, as the actor, Peter Ustinov, points out, "Since we are destined to live out our lives in the prison of our mind, our one duty is to furnish it well."[23]

Assisted Forms of Relaxation

Audiotapes

Relaxation is something you can always do on your own with no help from anyone. But there are also several ways you can seek relaxation with the help of professionals. If you'd like to use visualization to relax for longer periods of time, for example, you might want to use audio tapes as an aid in doing this. Guided visualizations are available on tapes that take you through relaxing scenes for ten or twenty minutes. Most tapes include someone talking to you to help you relax, and some include sounds like waves or music in the background. In the Helpful Resources section at the end of the book, you will find a list of relaxation tapes with ordering information. Tapes can be especially helpful when your mind seems too filled with thoughts to relax. Focusing on someone's voice giving you instruction allows you to occupy your mind while relaxing.

Biofeedback

One type of assisted relaxation that has been scientifically proven to be very effective for pain and stress relief is biofeedback. Biofeedback is a machine-assisted form of relaxation training. It is based on our ability to learn control over bodily responses. Biofeedback allows us to perceive our responses and learn skills to regulate them.

Biofeedback is best learned in a practitioner's office. (See Helpful Resources for help in finding a practitioner in your area.) Depending on what symptoms you are having, the practitioner attaches sensors to your body typically on your hands, fingers, and forehead while you relax in a chair. These sensors measure various physiological functions such as your heart rate, blood pressure, skin resistance, muscle tension, hand temperature, and brain wave activity. The instruments translate these body functions into both sound and video images. You can see your responses on a computer screen continuously while you are being monitored (see Figure 6.5). You can also hear the measurements, such as your heart rate, coming from the computer as a tone. This feedback gives you electronically enhanced information about how your body is operating.

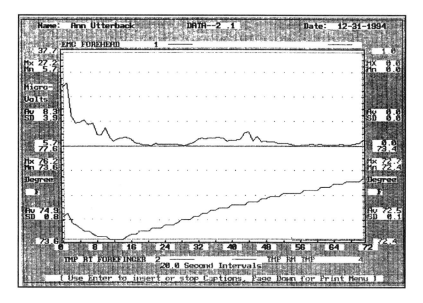

Figure 6.5 During a 24-minute period, relaxation is evidenced by decreasing muscle tension in the forehead (top line on the graph) and increasing hand temperature (bottom line).

(Figure provided by Karen Kverno, Ph.D., Director of Biofeedback and Behavioral Therapies, Medical Illness Counseling Center, Chevy Chase, MD.)

In a typical session, the biofeedback practitioner puts the sensors in place and then assists you in relaxing by using a relaxation technique such as you have read about in this chapter. As you relax you will be able to see and hear the responses happening in your body as you look and listen to the computer. You will then have tangible feedback to help you learn the Relaxation Response.

Hand warming is one of the best measures of relaxation. When I tried biofeedback for migraine headaches, I discovered that by concentrating on warming my hands, I actually decreased the tension in my face. A computer tone let me know when the temperature of my hands was increasing. I found I could change the tone voluntarily. This meant that by warming my hands I was relaxing my facial muscles and my entire body. Biofeedback helped me understand the body-mind connection in a very concrete way.

Biofeedback also gives you a sense of control. You begin to feel that you can take control of the stress that at times may seem so out of control. This is especially helpful when you have pain as a result of your stress in conditions such as migraines, tension headaches, muscle spasms, or gastrointestinal disorders. It is also effective with insomnia, anxiety, panic disorders, hypertension, phobias, and tics or tremors.

Biofeedback training takes several sessions with the equipment to teach you the ways you can alter your internal response to stress. Once this is learned, you can use these same skills without the equipment. You will learn what total relaxation feels like and how to achieve it. This will allow you to sense the subtle signs of stress in your body so you can use your relaxation techniques to stop the stress before it escalates.

Massage

If you want to experience relaxation without having to be an active participant, you might want to try massage. Massage has been recognized for over 3000 years as a healing and relaxing technique that revitalizes the body and mind. All you have to do is lie down, and someone else takes charge of relaxing your body for you.

Many types of massage are available for stress control. These include deep tissue massage, Swedish massage (perhaps the most relaxing), and Shiatsu to name just a few. The purpose of all massage is to ease muscle tension, improve circulation, and promote balance in your body. Massage helps you identify areas of your body where you tend to hold stress and tension. There is also new evidence that massage may actually improve your immune cell functions.[24]

The most apparent benefit of massage is that it makes you feel wonderful. A client told me that she had to get weekly massages after a traffic accident. Now she says that if she had the money she would get a massage every day. Most people agree. There is no better way to honor yourself and take time to relax than with a massage.

This importance of feeling wonderful was explained by Jim Vance, a veteran television anchor in Washington, D.C. He explained, "In the news business we approach what is really hopelessness on a daily basis with what we cover. It's important to luxuriate in the other side."[25]

Look for a massage therapist with whom you feel comfortable and one you trust. This will help you relax completely during your massage. In the Helpful Resources section, you will find the telephone number for the National Certification Board for Therapeutic Massage & Bodywork. You can call there to locate a certified massage therapist near you whether you are at home or traveling. To find a massage therapist with the best training, look for one who is nationally certified in therapeutic massage and body work and is also a member of the American Massage Therapy Association.

If you want a mini-massage, you might consider something as simple as getting a facial. Whether you're male or female, a facial will give you an hour or so of a relaxing treatment that will also help your skin. This can be especially beneficial if you're an on-air television anchor or reporter who wears make-up regularly. A monthly facial can do wonders for your complexion and your stress level.

One client told me she enjoys the simple relaxation time she gets during her visit to the hairdresser's each month. She said she loves to read the magazines there that she'd never buy. She knows that during her time there no one can reach her and the pressures of the business are gone. This is another time when someone is caring for you. If you make the most of this time, you can use it as a relaxation break.

Yoga

A wonderful way to combine physical exercise with relaxation is by doing yoga. The philosophy and practice of yoga began more than 4000 years ago. One form of yoga called, "hatha yoga," combines breathing with stretching. In its more advanced forms it includes the study of a philosophy that promotes self-analysis and spirituality. The word, "yoga," comes from Sanskrit and means to "yoke" or "bring together and make whole." Practicing the gentle stretches of yoga that are combined with breathing can help you achieve balance and wholeness.

Dr. Dean Ornish includes yoga as a main component in his program for reversing heart disease. He points out that "We are often more aware of what is going on *around* us than what is going on *inside* us."[26] Yoga can help focus attention on our inner being and what's happening for us physically, emotionally, and spiritually. By doing this we can learn ways to relieve the stresses that affect us.

The practice of yoga requires no special equipment. You can work with a yoga teacher, attend a yoga class, or learn some of the yoga stretches from one of the many books on the subject (see Chapter 9, Suggested Reading). The beginning moves will be much like the stretching exercises described in Chapter 4 of this book. But when doing yoga, the emphasis is on combining your breathing with movement. Yoga stretches are often called poses because you move so slowly and with such emphasis on breathing. This is what makes the practice of yoga such an effective stress relieving activity.

Psychotherapy

One final way to participate in assisted relaxation is by working with a therapist who specializes in stress reduction. This might be a social worker or psychologist. Many people would rather go to their internist and get a prescription for a tranquilizer than pursue therapy. But medication will only help the symptoms of stress. This will bring temporary relief, but if you stop taking the medication the problem will still be there.

You don't have to be "crazy" to go to a therapist to get some help with your stress level. Many of my clients have found that short-term therapy, which might consist of eight or ten visits, can be very effective. One advantage of going to see a therapist is that it makes you set aside time to look at your stress level and learn how to alleviate it. That gives you a sense of control over your problems.

We often use our friends or spouses as therapists when that is not their job. I suggest to clients that they monitor how much time they spend complaining to others about their stress level, or how things are not going well for them at work. If you find that that is the main thing you talk to others about, you might consider asking a professional to take that burden. Having someone who will really listen and will assist you in dealing with stress, means you can interact with friends in a different way. So don't be afraid to ask for help with your stress. In the Helpful Resources section (Chapter 8) you'll find telephone numbers of associations that can help you find a therapist in your area. Having someone really listen to you is a wonderful gift to give yourself.

There are many avenues you can pursue to have some assistance in dealing with stress. One might work for you at one time while later you might want to turn to another technique. But learning to relax by using any of the means described in this chapter will teach you many things. You'll learn what triggers stress for you, and you'll find out where you hold that stress in your body. The techniques you use to relieve stress will give you control over pressures as they arise. As you practice relaxation, you'll learn that stress in your body can be a teacher to help you learn to adjust your life so that it works for you.

Healthy Suggestions

1 Breathing with the abdominal-diaphragmatic area is a natural stress reliever. Various postures and movements help you focus on this type of breathing because they force abdominal-diaphragmatic breathing. Try these activities and focus on the movement around your abdominal area, your sides, and your back. Some postures may work better for you than others. In all of them, concentrate on your breathing.

- Bend from the waist at a ninety degree angle letting your arms and head hang relaxed. Keep your knees slightly flexed. Remain in this position until you can feel your abdominal-diaphragmatic breathing.

- Sit forward in a chair and put your elbows on your knees. Breathe normally and focus attention on the location of the movement.

- Sit up straight on the front edge of a chair. Drop your arms and grab the legs of the chair to lock your shoulders in place so they cannot rise. Push your abdominal area out as you breathe.

- Tilt your head back and yawn deeply. Feel the movement in your abdominal area. This is an excellent way to relax the throat.

One of the best postures for feeling abdominal-diaphragmatic breathing is lying down. Find a comfortable carpet or bed and stretch out on your back. Spread your legs slightly and move your arms away from your body so that there is open space in your armpits. Perform the following activities:

- Close your eyes and concentrate on your breathing.

- Place your right hand on your chest and your left hand on your abdomen. Notice that you can keep your right hand still while your left hand rises and falls with the breath.

- Place a book on your abdomen and watch it rise as you inhale and fall as you exhale.

You can work with a partner, to help you focus on abdominal-diaphragmatic breathing. Stand opposite your partner and put your hand on your partner's abdominal area just above the waist. Ask your partner to inhale and push your hand away. Focus on the movement of the abdominal area. Switch tasks. If either of you has difficulty, forget about breathing and simply push the hand away. Concentrate on moving those muscles, and then put an inhalation with the movement. (These exercises and others are available in my book, *Broadcast Voice Handbook.* See order information at the end of this book.)

2 Stephen Levine offers a way to improve breathing and relaxation by softening the belly. The simple act of inhaling deeply enough so that the belly expands is the beginning of achieving a soft belly. It means letting go of the armoring we use to protect ourselves. His soft belly guided meditation is available in his book, *Guided Meditations, Explorations and Healings* (see Chapter 9, Suggested Reading). You can also order a tape of the guided soft belly meditation from Warm Rock Tapes (call 800-731-HEAL).

If you want to pursue relaxation into the area of meditation, Levine gives a wonderful introduction to meditation in his book, *A Gradual Awakening* (see Suggested Reading). A book by Stephen Levine, *A Year To Live,* offers a plan for pursuing meditation and spirituality for a 365-day period. This can give you a deep understanding of the benefits of incorporating relaxation into your life.

3 There are many ways to use breathing for relaxation. Try a few of these and see which ones work for you. They work best with your eyes closed.

- Concentrate on the coolness of the air as you inhale through the nose, and the warmness as you exhale.

- Pause for two seconds between your inhalation and exhalation. Let yourself relax into that time of non-breathing.

- Count your inhalations up to five. When you reach five begin again.

- Imagine tension flowing out of your body as you exhale.

- Concentrate on your stomach expanding as you inhale and contracting as you exhale.

- After you've concentrated on your breath for a few minutes, turn your attention to another part of your body like your hands or feet. Simply feel how they feel as you are breathing.

- Imagine you're breathing in one color of air and exhaling another color. Breathe in blue and breathe out yellow.

- Concentrate on internal things like your breathing and any tension you might feel. Then switch your focus to outside your body. What do you hear? First listen to the most obvious sounds like talking or a television and then listen for the subtle sounds like a clock ticking or a bird singing. Feel your body sitting in the chair. What air temperature do you feel around you? Let yourself switch back and forth between your inner world and outer world.

4 Using walking to relax can have lots of benefits. First, you get some exercise. Next you are breathing cleaner air (hopefully). And finally, you are relaxing. To really relax when walking, try to stay very focused when you walk. You might start out by counting your steps. Next, turn your focus to what your feet feel like as they walk. How does the surface you're walking on feel? How does your foot feel in the shoe? And then expand your focus to the sounds you hear around you. Focus first on the very obvious sounds, and then try and hear the subtle, soft sounds. This focus will help you relax.

5 If visualization seems like a foreign experience to you, try these suggestions:

- Imagine you're biting into a lemon. Feel the response in your body.

- Imagine you're just waking up from a restful sleep. Feel how relaxed your body is.

- Imagine the fire alarm just went off. Sense how your body tenses.

- Imagine you're in your mother's kitchen or the kitchen of a friend you visit often. Can you smell the food? Can you see the kitchen clearly in your mind?

As you experiment with these activities, note which senses you tend to use the most. Do you see things in your mind mostly or do you smell or feel them?

6 For many of us, illness is the only time we slow down enough to really relax. It's our only time out. Dr. Bernie Siegel has said that illness is the body's "reset button."[27] It gives us a chance to evaluate our life and begin again. Rather than waiting to get ill to experience that, imagine that you are ill. Let's say you have the flu but the worst of your symptoms have passed. You're too sick to work, but not too sick to do some other things that are relaxing. How are you spending your days? Make a list of what you do when you're sick that allows you to relax. It might be reading a novel or looking at magazines or sleeping. Give yourself permission to do these things when you're not sick.

7 Edmund Jacobsen refined a series of more than 200 exercises that relax muscles throughout the body in a progressive manner. He called it, appropriately, "progressive relaxation." He said, "An anxious mind cannot exist within a relaxed body."[28] Progressive relaxation takes you step by step through your body, tensing and relaxing muscles. You can find scripts for guided progressive relaxation sessions in many of the books on relaxation found in the Suggested Reading section of this book (Chapter 9). There are also audiotapes described in the Helpful

Resources section (Chapter 8) that guide you through progressive relaxation.

8 Imagine what it would be like not to be stressed. What would you do if you had a day to yourself to be completely relaxed? Would you get a massage? Would you take a long walk? Make a list of these things. Imagine that you can "waste time" without any regard to being productive. What else would you add to the list? Going to a baseball game or a movie? Reading a novel? Playing tennis? Taking a long, leisurely drive? Design a day for yourself that would be totally relaxing. Instead of saying to yourself, "What needs to be done next?" let yourself focus on, "What do I *want* to do now?"

One client told me she likes to check into a hotel for a night a few times a year to get away from everything. She asks her husband to care for the children, and she doesn't leave the number at the hotel with anyone but him (and only to be used in dire emergency). During her evening, she soaks in a hot tub, orders room service, and watches a movie or reads a novel in complete relaxation. You can, of course, do this at home by turning off your phone, pager, fax machine, and television. Not being "on call" can have a very relaxing effect.

When you start putting more relaxing activities into your day, you may feel some resistance about it. Many times, as Stephen Levine points out, "We become like the rooster who thinks his crowing makes the sun come up each morning."[29] When we actually take some time away from all the demands that plague us, we may be surprised to find that life can go on without us. This realization may help reduce stress as well. Remember that the more balanced your life is, the more productive you can be. It's not a luxury to relax and have down time. It's a necessity.

9 Participating in religious or spiritual activities also has been shown to have a relaxing effect on the body. Dr. Herbert Benson and other doctors have found that a person's religious commitment "is consistently associated with better health. The greater a person's religious commitment, the fewer psychological symptoms, the better the general health, the lower the blood pressure and the longer the survival. ...Religious commitment brings with it a lifetime of benefits."[30] Many studies have shown that prayer is one of the best forms of relaxation. It quiets the body, focuses thoughts, and provides optimism. Attending a church service also includes these components as well as relaxing music, beautiful surroundings, and an opportunity to socialize in a relaxed manner. If you feel inclined to do so, you might expand your involvement in religious or spiritual endeavors.

10 Here's a quick relaxer you can use if you find your stress level getting out of control:

Step One: If possible, find a quiet spot away from the chaos around you. Go into the restroom or walk away from the situation you're in for a few minutes.

Step Two: Do some gentle stretching to relax your body. Rotate your shoulders slowly and reach up over your head as if you were picking apples off a tree.

Step Three: Place your hands on your abdomen just above your waistband and take a deep abdominal-diaphragmatic breath. As you exhale, imagine the stress flowing out of your body with the breath.

Step Four: Take three more breaths as slowly and completely as you can. Focus on your breathing, pausing slightly between the inhalation and exhalation.

Step Five: Visualize yourself going back into the event you just left feeling relaxed and refreshed.

11 Keep a record of the times when you have stress symptoms such as headaches, breathing difficulties, and/or an excess or lack of saliva when on-air. Arrange relaxation breaks around these times during your day. Also check your eating habits that might exacerbate stress (see Chapter 5). Design your day so you avoid stress symptoms before they start.

7

Avoiding Pitfalls

From the Newsroom:

Janet Evans, News Director/Anchor
KLBJ Radio, Austin, Texas

Broadcasters are used to being on deadlines. Our deadlines are not hour by hour. In radio, they can be second by second. It's really a combat mentality. As the morning reporter, I get up at 3:00 a.m. to get to work at 4:00 a.m. I think this is more stressful than a day schedule. There's a tendency for people who work this particular shift to overeat because your eating schedule is thrown upside down. I think you can gain weight and that can add to the frustration and stress. In any kind of shift work you have to think healthy. I drink a lot of water which is very cleansing for me. I also use a saline nasal spray probably three or four times a day. My sinus infections have gone down, and knock on wood, other people have had colds, and I haven't. We have a larger newsroom than most radio shops. We have cubicles with close working conditions, and we're sharing some space. Illnesses spread in these conditions. We're in a tight building, and we don't get a lot of fresh air. Our management has tinkered with the ventilation system. Every few years they have the ventilation system cleaned out. They have done everything they can to try to make it as healthy as possible. I like to keep my work area clean. If the janitorial staff doesn't wipe my desk area, I'll take a bottle of Lysol cleaner and do it myself. We wipe the microphones with Lysol regularly. I'm also an avid hand washer because I know that reduces infections. When I travel on an airplane, I use the saline spray before I go, and I take it in my purse. I carry a bottle of water with me. I drink that on the airplane and in the hotel. I always drink lots of water. It's easy when you're traveling to lose some of your healthy habits. I try to eat right, and rest as much as I can. I also build in some quiet time. I'm really past the stage where I want to talk on an airplane. That's my down time. I want to read, relax, and leave my work behind me. When I return, I used to go right back to work. Now I give myself an extra day off just to catch up and get ready for work. This is especially important with the shift I'm on. It's tough to go to bed by 7:30 or 8:00 p.m. It's not that you don't like your job, but it's depressing to know that you're going to bed before the rest of the world. I'm trying different techniques to stay healthy. I think for anyone who wants to have longevity in this business, you have to find ways to juggle lots of things. You have to manage to have a life — both private and profes-sional. It's difficult, but if you want to stay in this business, you have to figure out a way. In broadcasting, there are always challenges, and you can't stay in a state of perpetual upheaval.

Avoiding Pitfalls

*Identifying what you need and want may be more difficult
than you imagine. By getting caught up in meeting the
needs of others and giving them what they seem to want,
you probably have spent little time listening to yourself.*
Carmen Renee Berry[1]

It's difficult to think of your own needs when you work in a business as stressful as broadcasting. Taking care of your body may get lost in the day to day stresses of getting the news out. But protecting your body from things like colds, cigarette smoke, and unhealthy work situations should be a top priority. If you don't keep yourself healthy, you have little to give to your job.

The Common Cold

"Help! My anchor has had a cold for two weeks, and it's getting worse. What can I do?" I receive questions like this whenever I give a lecture or visit a station. Most of us suffer from some voice problems when we have a cold, but if you're on-air this may be a special challenge. As one news director explained, "Reporters and anchors who don't sound like themselves are no good to the station. We even get complaints from viewers."

Whether you're on-air or you have another position in the newsroom, it's hard to know what to do when you have a cold. Even though most of us suffer from an average of two colds a year, confusion abounds about how to treat a cold. It is helpful to know a little about what causes a cold so that you can deal with it the best way possible.

What Is a Cold?

A cold is a natural response to an invading virus. It usually takes over a week for the immune system to attack and contain the virus. What makes us feel miserable are the symptoms associated with the process of the body healing itself. The symptoms we hate are actually signs that our immune systems are working.

The first symptom is often a sore throat caused by the tissue swelling once the virus has taken hold. This swelling makes vocal production difficult and limits resonance. It feels like you're tearing up your throat when you talk with a sore throat, and that's usually what's happening. It's important to protect the tissue when it's vulnerable by talking as little as possible.

Next the vocal tract becomes flooded with mucus which is the body's natural flushing agent to move the virus out of the throat and nose and into the stomach to be killed. For an on-air person, this is often the most distressing symptom because it may block the nose, creating a denasal voice and flood the throat, causing coughing. A cough is a vicious assault on the vocal folds with the air moving at over 100 miles per hour. This assault can irritate the vocal folds causing possible hoarseness and/or laryngitis.

Other cold symptoms have less effect on the voice but make working difficult. There is a general fatigue that comes with most colds which is the body's way of shutting off all functions that are not essential to fighting the virus. We may also develop a fever which actually has a positive function. Viruses thrive at 85 degrees or lower.[2] Fever creates an inhospitable environment for the virus to reproduce. It is helpful to tolerate a fever up to 100 degrees for the first three days of a cold. Anything higher or lasting longer should get medical attention. See an internist or otolaryngologist (ear, nose, and throat doctor) if any symptoms persist beyond two weeks or if there is sudden, severe hoarseness or laryngitis.

Causes of Colds and Flu

Colds are caused by over 200 specific viral strains from eight different viral groups. The cold virus is one of the most primitive forms of life. It causes multiple symptoms that develop over the life of the cold. Bacteria, on the other hand, do not cause colds or flu, but they cause isolated secondary problems like sinus or ear infections and strep throat. Only bacterial infections which attack cells from the outside can be killed by antibiotics. Viruses live and work inside cells where the antibiotics do not reach.[3] Our only recourse with a cold is to treat the symptoms.

The flu is also caused by a virus, but it is a different virus than the common cold. The symptoms of the flu are different as well. The flu usually hits suddenly unlike the slow progression of a cold. The flu often begins with high fever (102 to 104 degrees), muscle aches, and extreme fatigue. Respiratory symptoms may not be apparent until later, and they may be accompanied by intestinal distress. The flu usually keeps a person in bed for three days or more, and that may be followed by weeks of fatigue.

The flu virus is spread much more easily than a cold virus. Air-borne droplets that are contaminated by the flu virus move through the air which means it's difficult to protect yourself against infection. One cough may disperse germs as much as thirteen feet. Fortunately, there are fewer flu viruses than cold viruses, and a flu shot can be very effective in protecting you each year against the latest flu virus.

Treatment for Colds

Cold symptoms should be treated with care, but it's often confusing which symptom you should treat. You want to dry out your nose when you have a cold so you'll sound better and breathe more easily. But when you dry your nasal passages, you dry your throat as well. A dry throat is an invitation for vocal damage.

Drying your mucous membranes also limits the healing effect of the mucus. The nose and throat are lined with tiny hairs called cilia. These hairs are like seaweed that flagellate to move mucus, dust, and viruses out of the vocal area. If these cilia become dry they harden like coral, and the mucus becomes stagnant. This is a breeding ground for bacteria which can cause a secondary infection. So it is important to let the mucus do its work as much as possible even though this is not comfortable and makes talking more difficult.

The best advice, supported by an advisory panel of the Food and Drug Administration,[4] is to use single-symptom, over-the-counter medications to treat cold symptoms as they occur. Since the symptoms usually appear serially, you do not need to treat all of them at once. Americans spend over one billion dollars a year on multi-symptom cold formulas, but many include ingredients you do not need like caffeine and alcohol. In fact, some liquid cold formulas have a 25 percent alcohol content which is twice the percentage found in many wines and more than half that found in 80-proof liquor.[5] Also, multi-symptom cold formulas often do not have enough dosage of individual drugs to give relief. Treating each symptom will give you more control over treatment and will help protect your vocal tract.

A simple decongestant can be used to limit mucus production when it causes difficulty with on-air work or makes you too miserable. Decongestants clear blocked nasal passages by limiting the flow of blood in the nose and throat. Most multi-symptom cold medications include antihistamines which fight an allergic reaction, not a cold. Antihistamines will do more harm than good for broadcasters because the drying effect may cause increased hoarseness. They may also thicken mucus, causing a simple cold to progress into a bacterial infection.

When mucus production is a problem, stick to a single drug decongestant like Sudafed. This contains only pseudoephedrine. Be cautious with decongestion nasal sprays because of the rebound effect caused when the medication wears off and the tissue swells. They can become addictive in the vicious cycle to keep the nasal passages open. A decongestant spray can be helpful, however, if you have to fly with a cold. Use the spray one hour before take-off and again one hour before landing. If you're especially congested, take a decongestant pill as well one hour before take-off and again as soon as the dosage instructions suggest.

One nasal spray that is helpful is a non-medicinal saline spray like Ocean or NaSal. This liquid helps restore moisture to the mucus membranes keeping the cilia functioning. It can be used as many times a day as necessary. A salt water solution can also be used to gargle. Gargling with warm salt water may soothe a sore throat, but it only reaches the back of the throat, not the vocal folds. Gargling may dry the vocal folds because of the air that is forced up to produce the gargling. Gargle if it soothes your throat, but keep your fluid intake up to help moisten the vocal folds.

If aches and fever inhibit on-air work, take a pain reliever like ibuprofen or acetaminophen. Avoid aspirin because it may increase the likelihood of a vocal fold hemorrhage.

If coughing becomes excessive, a cough suppressant with expectorant like Robitussin DM can help. This thins mucus allowing it to be coughed up easily. Coughing serves the purpose of clearing the lungs, so if it is not excessive and does not keep you awake at night, try to live with it. Coughing can be harmful to the throat, however, and broadcasters should see a doctor if coughing is severe or if it lasts more than two weeks.

The advice you read in Chapter 5 about drinking water applies even more when you have a virus. Drinking plenty of decaffeinated fluids is important to keep the viscosity of the mucus at the right level. Warm fluids like decaffeinated tea or chicken soup may be soothing to the throat. Remember to consume at least one-half ounce of decaffeinated fluids per pound of body weight daily.

Later in this chapter you'll read about the importance of keeping a good humidity level. It's important to have a high level of humidity when you have a cold. It should be between 40 and 60 percent. Using a warm-air humidifier in your bedroom is very helpful. Do not use a cool mist humidifier because it may promote the growth of infectious allergens.[6] And avoid smoking because one cigarette can paralyze cilia for as long as thirty or forty minutes. This makes it easier for a smoker to get sick in the first place and for a viral infection to become a more severe bacterial infection.[7] Remember, too, that rest and sleep are the major ways that cells revitalize. This is why rest is so important when a virus strikes.

As you read in Chapter 2, stress lowers our immune system. A psychologist at Carnegie-Mellon University, Dr. Sheldon Cohen, found that people who tested as having a high stress level were twice as likely to catch a cold as those who were under low stress.[8] Resting and relaxing will protect you against colds and help you recover faster if you have one.

Research is showing that the use of zinc gluconate lozenges may shorten the length of a cold from an average of 7.6 days to 4.4 days and reduce the symptoms of sore throat, coughing, nasal congestion, and hoarseness.[9] I have found this to be true if I start using the lozenges at the first sign of a cold. You might want to consult your doctor or pharmacist about the use of these lozenges.

Avoiding Colds

Most of us think that as winter approaches, the cold season is upon us. Old wives' tales tell us we shouldn't get our feet wet or go out in the cold air without a hat. Actually, these things have nothing to do with catching a cold. Colds come from viruses that are around all year long. We get a cold from someone who is infected. If they are carrying a virus to which we have no immunity, we get the virus. We get more colds in the winter because more of us are trapped in enclosed spaces where viruses can be transferred. This is especially true of school children who often start the process by bringing viruses home. Also, the air is dryer outdoors and indoors in the winter, and this dries out our mucous membranes, making us more susceptible to colds.

What can you do to avoid the outbreak of a cold virus in the newsroom? Since we shed cold viruses for up to three days into a cold, one thing to do is to stay home when you feel the first symptoms of a cold coming on. The rest you'll get will help you fight the cold, and you'll protect others from your virus.

It also helps to be aware of how the virus is spread. Cold viruses enter our bodies primarily through our noses and eyes. We pick up the viruses on non-porous surfaces like telephones, keyboards, microphones, and doorknobs. Viruses can live on these surfaces for hours and, in some cases, weeks if it is a moist area. Any surface that is touched by lots of people is a potential carrier. We touch these surfaces and then our faces and allow the viruses to enter our bodies.

To avoid infection, we need to keep our hands clean and avoid touching our faces. Both of these things are hard to do. Frequent hand washing when colds are around the newsroom will help. Use a disinfectant, anti-bacterial soap if you can, but plain water will eliminate some germs. Also use a disinfectant like Lysol, Pine Sol, or alcohol to keep frequently touched surfaces clean.

Cleanliness is important even when you're home with a cold because you can reinfect yourself. Throw away used tissues, and replace hand towels often. It's also a good idea to get a new toothbrush once you are over the worst of your symptoms since the dampness of a toothbrush can breed infection. And if someone else in your home has a cold, there is a 40 percent chance you will get it.[10] Therefore, it is important to use precaution at home as well as in the newsroom.

Is Your Newsroom Making You Sick?

I am often amazed when I visit news operations and see the conditions under which many broadcasters work. I am not talking about the noise and confusion that are a part of any newsroom. I am talking about unhealthy environmental conditions that go unnoticed. One newsroom I visited was being completely remodeled while the on-air talent worked around the construction. The construction dust was so thick it was possible to write on most of the surfaces in the newsroom. The computers had been carefully draped with plastic, but the most expensive equipment in the newsroom, the vocal tracts of the on-air staff, was unprotected. The news director voiced concern that so many of his anchors and reporters were ill, and yet no one connected the illnesses with the construction.

Another newsroom had recently completed renovation and had a beautiful work space to show for it. What had been ignored, however, was the placement of the air vents. Both the lead anchors had desks positioned directly below air conditioning vents. Again there was no association made between their bouts of hoarseness and laryngitis and this unhealthy design.

Sick Building Syndrome

Most of us recognize major hazards like these construction problems, and we have heard about the well-publicized threats of radon and asbestos. But building problems do not have to be this severe to cause significant vocal and health problems.

The overall health of the working environment has become an area of increasing concern. The World Health Organization in 1993 estimated that 30 percent of this nation's four million commercial buildings had poor indoor-air quality. The term, "sick building syndrome," was coined, which is used when there are unexplained respiratory problems, excessive fatigue, headaches, and/or eye irritations experienced by 10-20 percent of a building's occupants at a given time.

This syndrome has special significance for the health of broadcasters. All of the associated symptoms can be potentially harmful to vocal production and add to a person's stress level. Nose and throat irritation and sinus discomfort affect resonance. They also cause changes in the mucosal lubrication of the vocal tract which can cause vocal damage. Respiratory problems and lethargy affect vocal energy. Headaches and eye irritation make concentration difficult. While these problems might be uncomfortable conditions for a worker in another type of office, in a newsroom they are career damaging. Despite this, little concern has been given to sick building syndrome in the broadcasting industry.

Thousands of low-level pollutants fill the air. Indoor chemical toxins include paint, cleaning and office machine chemicals, commercial pesticides, off-gassing from new rugs and upholstery, and cigarette smoke. Negligent maintenance of heating and air conditioning systems makes the problem worse. Unclean systems may become breeding grounds for building-related airborne illnesses like Legionnaire's Disease or Pontiac Fever.

In most buildings built or remodeled during the 1970s or '80s, there is not enough circulating outdoor air to dilute and remove contaminants.[11] Windows are often inoperable making it difficult to get natural ventilation. Working in an environment like this for hours at a time can be harmful. It is much the same effect as sitting on an airplane for eight hours and breathing stale, dry air. Pollutants and germs are allowed to recirculate creating an unhealthy environment. Carbon dioxide levels may also rise causing drowsiness, headaches, and decreased energy.

The pollution problem may even originate outside of the immediate office area. In a large building, poor ventilation will circulate polluted air from other offices where activities such as printing or painting may be taking place. This is also a problem when smoking is allowed in certain areas of a building. Fortunately, within the last five years most newsrooms have become smoke-free zones. But without good air ventilation, a newsroom staff may be inhaling smoke from another part of the building. In the next section of this chapter, you'll learn more about the hazards of secondhand smoke.

Other pollutants can cause problems as well. One newsroom I visited was situated next to a large parking garage, and the smell of car exhaust fumes was pervasive throughout the newsroom.

Indoor air pollution also happens when building managers shut down outside dampers in an attempt to save money on heating and air conditioning. Without proper circulation, newsroom air becomes a mixture of thousands of pollutants that are destructive to vocal health.

Common pollutants are the tiny mineral fibers in ceiling tiles and in the insulation that lines most ventilation systems. These tiny fibers are attracted to electrostatic fields generated by equipment like computer monitors. In a room with poor air ventilation, each computer screen attracts a pool of pollutants. Working in front of a screen puts news-room personnel in the worst possible place for clean air.

The concern of workers about indoor air quality has spawned litigation and prompted government agencies to take the matter seriously. The EPA is scheduled to release guidelines for indoor air quality. OSHA has drafted some proposed rules for indoor air quality, but it will take time for them to be adopted. Right now the standards are taken from the American Society of Heating, Ventilating, and Air-Conditioning Engineers. But none of these standards takes into account the special needs of on-air broadcasters and other newsroom personnel.

Comfort Range Guidelines

Until clearer standards are adopted, the best approach for newsroom personnel is to become aware of the situation in your workplace. News directors should check the build-ing lease if that applies. Most leases have what are called "Comfort Range Guidelines" which outline acceptable of-fice temperatures and humidity levels as well as how much outside air per square foot should be provided.

Average office temperatures for an ideal office environ-ment should be between 73 and 79 degrees with 30 percent to 60 percent humidity. It is relatively easy to monitor the tem-perature and humidity using a thermometer with a hygrom-eter. If the building fails to meet these standards, the building manager should be contacted. It is important to check the temperature and humidity in the studio and sound booths in addition to the newsroom. If there is a suspicion of sick building syndrome, it is worth the investment to bring in an outside consultant to check the air quality (see Chapter 8, Helpful Resources). The EPA also provides free information on indoor air quality from its Public Information Center in Washington, D.C. (see Helpful Resources).

If the square footage of an area is not too large, the in-stallation of free-standing warm-air ultrasonic humidifiers can improve humidity levels. Several newsrooms have installed humidifiers, and the news directors have reported fewer sore throats and colds during the winter from all the staff and generally healthier voices from those on air. Humidifiers do need to be maintained and cleaned frequently to avoid recreating an unhealthy air environment. I caution broadcasters and news directors not to use the units unless they are committed to cleaning them as described in the instructions for each unit.

Air filtering devices that contain high-efficiency particulate arrestors are also beneficial. These devices can be especially helpful in an enclosed space like a sound booth. If the area is poorly ventilated, the device can be run at all times except when someone is on the air so that the air stays filtered and clean. It is also important to keep sound booths vacuumed and dusted. These rooms are often not included in regular office cleaning, and they can become stale, dirty spaces that contribute to vocal problems.

Another fairly inexpensive way to improve air quality in the newsroom is to use plants as an air freshening mechanism. Living plants are more than just decoration. They provide added humidity and filter the air. It is important, however, that they be of the correct type and number for your newsroom. Working with a local nursery or gardening service can ensure that the plants become a healthy part of the newsroom environment. But, like the humidifier, they need to be properly maintained so that they do not become breeding grounds for more pollutants.

Smoking

No single environmental hazard comes close to the devastation done by cigarette smoke. In fact, every year since 1964, the Surgeon General has identified smoking as the single most important preventable cause of death in our society.[12] Most doctors agree that the best thing you can do for your health is not to smoke. Smokers lose an average of 15 years of life.[13]

The harmful effects of smoking are much more widely known now than they were even five years ago. You can't work in the news business and not know of the harmful effects of smoking. But when the first cigarettes (Camels) were manufactured in 1913, they were actually used to avoid the health hazard of spitting chewing tobacco which many feared spread tuberculosis. At that time, lung cancer was not even officially registered as a disease. That didn't happen until 27 years later when cigarettes had begun to take their toll.[14] Since that time, cancers related to smoking have become a major health problem.

The magnitude of the problem is strongly related to the fact that smoking is not an easy habit to break. All of my clients who smoke know the health hazards, but the process of quitting is never easy. Studies have shown that the addiction is so strong that monkeys who can push a lever to be given injections of nicotine instead of food will continue to push the lever until they die of starvation.[15] Many scientists think that nicotine is more addictive than heroin or crack cocaine.[16]

When you inhale a cigarette, you're inhaling over 4000 chemical compounds including at least 43 different carcinogenic substances.[17] And the effects of the inhalation reach your brain in six seconds, which is twice as fast as an injection of heroin.[18]

Dr. Dean Ornish has studied how smokers control their moods with the chemicals in cigarettes. Short, quick puffs or low doses tend to arouse the brain's functions while long drags or high doses slow it down. So smokers can use a cigarette to stimulate or calm themselves.[19] The stimulation comes from the effect nicotine has on the adrenal glands.

Nicotine may quadruple the amount of adrenaline in the body.[20]

The carcinogens in cigarettes are very harmful to the body. Cancers of the lung, mouth, pharynx, larynx, esophagus, cervix, kidney, bladder, and pancreas are strongly associated with smoking. In fact, smoking accounts for 30 percent of all cancer deaths.[21] Lung cancer, always one of the main killers of men, has now grown among women as their smoking percentages have risen. In 1987 lung cancer surpassed breast cancer as the leading cause of cancer death among women.[22]

The American Cancer Society estimates that around 170,000 lives will be lost to cancer because of smoking each year.[23] But the total U.S. deaths related to smoking is estimated to exceed 419,000.[24] One reason for the additional deaths is that smoking causes more deaths from heart disease than from lung cancer in both men and women.[25] The toxins in tobacco affect the entire body.

As you read earlier in the chapter, smoking paralyzes the cilia in the nose, throat, and lungs. These little seaweed-like hairs should move back and forth about 900 times per minute to keep any solid pollutants moving out of the respiratory tract.[26] Smoking stops this process which forces the body to produce more mucus to take over the job of the cilia. This mucus produces the typical smoker's cough and lower pitched voice. This is not a voice to admire because it is a signal of an unhealthy vocal tract.

To my surprise, more than one female client has told me that her news director suggested all the women in the shop smoke to lower their pitch. That's like recommending that someone get drunk before they drive because they will be more relaxed. It's deadly advice. The lower pitch you hear in a smoker's voice is evidence of the damage smoking is doing.

Every cigarette a person smokes has a detrimental effect on the body. There is no threshold below which smoking ceases to increase the risk of lung cancer.[27] Even one cig-arette a day can increase the risk. Of course, the more you smoke the greater the hazards. A person smoking two or more packs per day, for example, has a 12 to 25 times greater risk of dying of lung cancer.[28] But smoking any cig-arettes in a day is harmful. This is especially true if you combine tobacco and alcohol. Many clients tell me they are only "social smokers," and the only time they smoke is when they're out for drinks. The combination of alcohol and tobacco greatly increases your cancer risks.

And you don't have to be the one smoking the cigarette to be in danger. Environmental smoke, or secondhand smoke, has been classified as a Group A carcinogen which puts it in the ranks of asbestos in terms of cancer-causing potential. The American Cancer Society reports that 4000 Americans die of lung cancer every year from secondhand smoke.[29] Any close association with a smoker increases your risk of lung cancer by 30 percent, and being married to a heavy smoker increases it by 70 percent according to the National Cancer Institute.[30]

If you do smoke, stop. It's imperative if you're an on-air broadcaster. (See Healthy Suggestion #3 for information on quitting.) The damage to your throat and your voice is a very real threat to your career. Anyone working in broad-casting should be aware of the dangers of smoking and sec-ondhand smoke. It's not really a gamble that you'll have problems if you inhale smoke. It's a reality.

If you stop smoking, you'll notice immediate benefits. Your throat will clear of mucus which will improve your voice. You will cough less which will protect your vocal folds. You will have fewer colds and respiratory infections. Food will taste better, and you may gain a few pounds. The weight gain is not a valid reason, however, to keep smoking. You can lose any excess weight with exercise (see Chapter 4). And the "Tufts University Diet & Nutrition Healthletter" re-ports that you have to gain 100 to 150 pounds to make your health risks as great as they are if you smoke.[31] So don't let the fear of a few pounds keep you smoking.

Some of the harmful effects of smoking will linger even after you stop. It takes 10 years for your lung cancer risk to return to normal after you stop smoking, and 15 years for your heart disease risk to drop to normal.[32] The rates begin to improve as soon as you quit, but because of the magnitude of the damage, the complete repair process is a slow one. But it's never too late to stop smoking, and you owe it to yourself. There are many pollutants we can't control, but inhaling cigarette smoke is not one of them.

Ergonomics

Environmental health includes more than just pollutants. Physical factors like desks, chairs, and monitors in a newsroom can cause harm as well.

When computers first began to be used in all newsrooms in the 1970s and 1980s, little thought was given to the effect they might have on the people using them. Computers were such a welcome addition to most broadcasters' lives, they relished spending time working on them versus the old typewriters. As more and more hours were logged at keyboards, however, repetitive stress injuries began to appear. Between 1978 and 1991, the reported cases of work-related repetitive stress injuries grew about sevenfold. In 1994, cases of disorders associated with repetitive stress injuries accounted for 65 percent of all occupational illnesses.[33] More and more people found that their work was injuring them. It was not unusual to see young writers or reporters wearing bandages or braces on their wrists from carpal tunnel injuries.

Because of situations like these, it has become important to know about ergonomics. This is the relationship between man and machine or the science of making your work area fit your body to allow your body to operate effectively and safely. Ergonomics involves looking at the viewing angles of monitors, the reach distances to equipment, and the comfort level of the person using the equipment. When these factors are adjusted, there is a reduction in fatigue, eye strain, and body discomfort. (See Figure 7.1.)

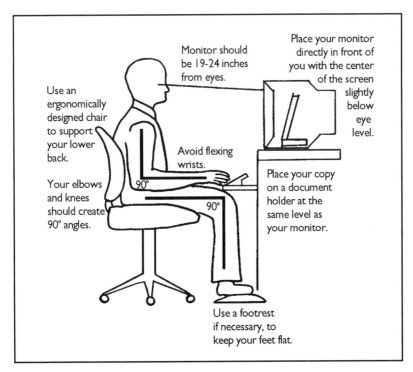

Figure 7.1 An ergonomically correct work space.

Eye Strain

One client of mine complained to me that she had started having awful headaches. When I asked her about their onset, she said they had begun when she switched from working overnights to days. As a writer, she spent most of her workday at the computer. What we discovered as we discussed her headaches was that the glare on her computer screen from a window near her desk, which had not been an issue at night, was the problem. The simple installation of an eye protection filter eliminated her headaches.

It's important to relax your eyes regularly as you work on a computer. Stop every fifteen minutes or so and blink a few times and focus your eyes on something about twenty feet away. This gives your eyes a rest. And if you can adjust the color on your monitor, use black characters with a light gray background for the least eye strain.

Placement of your monitor is important as well. Monitors should be 19 to 24 inches away from your eyes. The monitor should be directly in front of you on a horizontal plane with your eyes. The center of the screen should be slightly below your eye level. To test this, while seated at your desk extend your arm so it's parallel to your desktop. You should be touching the top of your screen if it is positioned correctly. If it's not correct, you may need to raise or lower your chair and/or your monitor.

This correct monitor position will help your eyes as well as your shoulder and neck muscles. Also place any copy that you are typing from at the same level as your monitor. It's easy to pull a neck muscle when you're looking down repeatedly at copy and up at the monitor.

Wrist and Arm Protection

The most common injury from computer work is carpal tunnel syndrome. This syndrome accounts for 43 percent of repetitive stress injuries and is growing at epidemic proportions in the workplace.[34] This injury occurs when there is repeated pressure on the median nerve in the wrist. The carpal tunnel is an area just below the heel of the hand through which nine finger tendons and the median nerve run. This nerve conducts impulses from the brain down the arm to the thumb, forefinger, middle finger, and half of the ring finger.[35] Repetitive up and down movements of the hands can cause the tendons to swell and put pressure on the nerve. Numbness and/or tingling can result.

To avoid carpal tunnel injury, bend your arms at a 90 degree angle and avoid any flexing of the wrists as you type. (See Healthy Suggestion #6 for more information about protecting your wrists.)

Avoiding Back Injuries

Back pain is an epidemic in America. Except for the common cold, it is the primary reason for missing work. Most newsroom personnel (excluding those who carry cameras) do not lift objects everyday that are heavy enough to cause back strain. But just sitting at a computer can injure your back. It is important to have an ergonomically designed chair that will support your lower back when working.

One adjustment that can help keep your back healthy is to use a foot rest with your chair. You can use a three-ring binder or a telephone book. Better still, purchase a foam or wooden foot rest that you can easily use at different chairs. This will improve your posture and protect your back.

I'm astonished at the horror stories I hear from anchors about the seating provided for them at the anchor desk. Many have told me they sit in chairs with backs that are broken or they have to sit on telephone books because the chairs will not adjust. This causes undue stress on both the body and the mind. A comfortable ergonomic chair is a small expense that will save money in the long run with fewer back aches and injuries.

Telephone Work

Muscular tension and stress tend to concentrate in our shoulders and necks. It's important to avoid holding your telephone between your ear and your shoulder when you need your hands free. If you talk on the phone for two hours or more a day, it's worth investing in a headset to use instead of holding the phone to your ear. Like a good chair, this is a small expense that will prevent neck and shoulder injuries.

Stretching is a good way to give your body a break when you're doing telephone work or just sitting and working at your desk for a long period. In Chapter 4 you'll find several good stretching methods that can be done right at your desk. These provide a break for your body, eyes, and mind.

Travel

Many times you may think that leaving the newsroom to go away on a trip will help your body and calm your stress. The idea of getting away from the daily stresses may be appealing, but even if the trip is for pleasure and not work, we often feel worse after a trip rather than better. In hotels and airplanes, the air is bad, the food may not be healthy, and exercising, especially on a work assignment, can be difficult.

Air Travel

One recent article sums up air travel well: "If people were meant to fly they'd have been born with wings and a small package of salted peanuts."[36] An airplane cabin does not offer much that supports health. One of the main reasons for this is the air quality inside the cabin.

To say that spending a few hours on a plane is like breathing desert air is giving air travel a good name. Most deserts have a humidity range of 20 to 25 percent. Airplane humidity has the amazingly dry level of 5 to 10 percent.[37] And the airline companies have no desire to make planes more humid because of the increased weight which means added expense as well as the risk of mold growth in the small, enclosed cabin of an airplane.

Altitude is one of the main reasons for the dry air on a plane. When you're flying at 35,000 feet, the altitude inside the plane is not what you left on the ground unless you live high up in the mountains. Most of the time you're cruising, the altitude inside the plane is around 7000 to 8000 feet.[38] This is dramatically higher than most of us are used to even if we live in the mile-high city of Denver. High altitude equals low humidity and this can result in a dry throat, greater risk of infection, and an overall lousy feeling.

Airlines will tell you that you're no more likely to catch a viral or bacterial infection on a plane than you would in any other enclosed space. But how many of us sit for five or more hours in a theater or church? And how many other enclosed spaces offer us so little humidity? When you combine the small space, a hundred or more people, and low humidity, you've got the perfect breeding ground for infection.

The Aviation Clean Air Act is before Congress as this book is going to press. This Act addresses the problem of poor air in airplanes. At the present time, many planes offer only 8 cubic feet of fresh air per minute per coach passenger. According to Rep. Jerrold Nadler, "The amount of fresh air allowed into the passenger cabin is left to the discretion of the pilot, who is required by the carrier to restrict the fresh air in order to conserve as much fuel as possible. 'Used' air is routinely recirculated through the cabin several times before fresh air is permitted to enter."[39]

The Aviation Clean Air Act, if passed, will increase the amount of fresh air to 20 cubic feet. This will be a big improvement especially if you travel coach. If you fly Business Class or First Class, you are already getting more air. This is not because the air is provided at a different ratio, but because there are fewer seats in these sections so fewer people breathe the air. In First Class now, for example, a person will receive around 50 cubic feet of air instead of the 8 in coach.[40]

Breathing dry, recirculated air is a special threat for on-air broadcasters. In Chapter 5 you read about the need for a moist vocal tract for a good on-air voice. Even a short flight for as little as two hours can wreak havoc on your throat.

On a plane you lose eight ounces of water by skin evaporation every hour.[41] This means when you fly from New York to L.A. you will lose forty ounces of water through your skin alone. That's as much as running an hour in 90 degree heat![42]

The body is over 60 percent water. The largest volume of water (around 75 percent) in our bodies is found within our cells. The rest is found outside the cells and as plasma in the blood. When we become dehydrated, the water in the cells may be affected. This may cause your muscles to become weak and fatigued.

Another factor that affects the water balance in our bodies is the amount of sodium we consume (see Chapter 5). Our bodies require a perfect balance of sodium and water to operate effectively. When we add sodium to our diets, as we would with those ubiquitous salted peanuts on the airplane, water is drawn out of the cells and blood to dilute the sodium. The more salt we consume, the more this will happen.

When you travel, it's easy to consume more sodium than you might at home. Let's suppose that when the drink cart comes by on the plane you decide that with your peanuts you'll have a can of bloody mary cocktail mix (without the alcohol which you know would be dehydrating). That adds a whopping 1910 milligrams of sodium to your body. Your daily maximum salt intake should be around 2400 milligrams. So with one airline snack you're approaching your entire day's supply. The sodium will make you retain more water since water always follows sodium. As the sodium in the body increases, more water stays in the body to balance it. This will add pounds and can cause swelling in your hands and feet.

So what can you do to avoid this trap? First, drink lots of water to combat the dehydration and balance any extra sodium. You should begin increasing your water intake several days before your flight. And on the plane, drink at least eight ounces every hour. Because the water on airplanes is not regulated, it is best to bring your own water. I never leave for a trip without a tall bottle of water. I always drink at least fifty ounces if I'm flying across the country.

Another thing you might want to try is a non-medicinal saline nasal spray to help keep your nose and throat moistened. You can read more about this in Healthy Suggestion #1 at the end of this chapter.

Airline food is notoriously bad not just because of the sodium content, but because of the taste as well. Meals are always prepared hours ahead of the flight and warmed in convection ovens on the plane. As the airlines cut expenses, the meals are getting smaller and are, at times, non-existent. When you do get a meal, it's likely to be loaded with sodium and fat.

There are two options for improving what you eat on the plane. One is to request a special meal. Over 4000 passengers a day on any given airline order special meals.[43] You must request these meals 24-hours in advance. Some of the healthiest are:

Cold or hot seafood plates
Fruit plates
Vegetarian meals
Low-salt meals

Bland meals (which might include a grilled chicken breast, rice, broccoli, cottage cheese with tomato, whole wheat bread, and angel food cake)

When you call to request a meal, the reservation agent or your travel agent can give you specific menus for each type of special meal. It is wise to check with the gate agent to be sure your meal is on the plane before departure.

If you want to drink something besides water with your meal, stay away from caffeine and alcohol (see Chapter 5), both of which have a dehydrating effect. Also watch out for drinks high in sodium like tomato juice. Orange juice is a good choice or decaffeinated coffee and sodas.

Another option to improve your diet on a plane is to take your own food. This allows you to eat whatever and whenever you choose. A stop at a deli for a sandwich, some yogurt, or containers of salad will usually offer you a healthier alternative than airline food. You might even find some healthy choices at the airport. Or you can bring food you've prepared like fruit, carrot or celery sticks, cheese, or a toasted bagel with some peanut butter or low-fat cream cheese on it. Other items to consider are instant low-fat, low-salt soups in a cup. Ask for hot water from the flight attendant for these. You can also use hot water to make drinks like hot chocolate or herbal tea that you bring. A little planning can make a big difference in your diet when you fly.

Once you get off the plane, watch the temptation to grab something to give you a lift with sugar and caffeine. Let's say you stop at Starbuck's for a quick snack as you're on your way to get your luggage at the airport. You buy a large coffee and a cinnamon scone. The coffee will give you 550 milligrams of caffeine which is more than twice the suggested daily intake. The scone weighs in at an amazing 530 calories or what you'd get with two pork chops and mashed potatoes with butter.[44] This quick snack is not a healthy one. You'll be especially tempted to grab this if you haven't eaten well on the plane.

Besides the dehydration and poor nutrition on an airplane, there are more health hazards to worry about. Ear problems are the biggest medical complaint of flying. Because of the rapid change of air pressure on take-off and landing, your ears may not adjust as they should. Your ears may feel one pressure on the outside and a different one on the inside. Chewing, swallowing, and yawning will usually alleviate this, but sometimes problems arise.

Problems are most likely to occur when you have a cold. With a cold, some fluid may be blocking the easy flow of air in and out of your eustachian tube. This is the time when you should use a decongestant pill and/or spray (as you read in the section on the common cold). It is recommended that you take a pill an hour before take-off and again an hour before landing if the first one has worn off. If you're especially congested, add a decongestant nasal spray as well at these times. It may take you a while to recover from the medication, but you'll be saved from the excruciating pain of a blocked ear.

Another problem that occurs on longer flights is back pain. Move around as much as possible while you fly. If you're drinking eight ounces of water every hour, you will no doubt get this exercise taking trips to the restroom. Do a little stretching while you're up and in your seat as well. Also use an airline pillow or rolled blanket behind your lower back while you're seated. Give your back a break by using your carry-on bag or briefcase as a footstool for some of the flight. Your knees should be slightly above your buttocks for the best back position.

Something that always helps me when I fly is an emergency comfort kit I always have in my carry-on bag. I have added items to this over the years until it contains what I need, and I keep it packed and ready to go all the time. I encourage you to take helpful items with you as well. Here's what my emergency comfort kit holds:

Airline Comfort Kit

Eye drops
Face and hand cream
Toothpaste and toothbrush
Saline nasal spray
Moist towlettes
Spray Evian water
Make-up
Any medications that might be needed

With this kit tucked away, I know I will be more comfortable flying. And if my luggage happens to get lost, I'll have most of what I need to get through a day.

Hotels and Restaurants

Unfortunately, the health challenges related to travel do not end when you leave the airport. You may have fairly unhealthy air in your hotel room as well. Forced air heating and air conditioning are standard, and often the hotel windows are sealed much like in high-rise office buildings. Except for long showers, there aren't many opportunities to increase the humidity level. Leaving the forced air unit off as much as possible will help. And, of course, continue drinking as much water as possible.

You may also find that it is more difficult to exercise when you're traveling. But if you're on a work assignment, this is the time you need it the most. When I travel, I always make sure I am staying at a hotel that has an exercise room. As difficult as it is, I get up an hour early and exercise before

I begin my work day. There's a service that can make this even easier. The Fitness Connection (see Helpful Resources section for the telephone number) is a free referral network that will locate a professional massage therapist, personal trainer, aerobic's instructor, health club, or spa for you wherever you travel. You can continue your exercise with the help of a professional even when you're traveling.

Another hazard that follows you off the plane is the difficulty of sticking to nutritious, low-fat, and low-salt meals. For example, if you decide to have a simple hamburger and onion rings at a restaurant like the Hard Rock Cafe, you may eat two day's worth of fat and a day's worth of calories in one meal. You'll get twice the fat of a McDonald's quarter-pounder and around 1050 milligrams of sodium.[45] Add a dessert to that, and you're literally off the scale.

To avoid this disaster of a meal, you can order fish or chicken with sauce on the side. A salad with oil and vinegar will also be low in calories and sodium. Watch out for soups which generally have a very high sodium content. Even the cheese crackers you might grab from a vending machine will hit you with 540 milligrams of sodium and 240 calories. A few dietary indiscretions can make a big difference in your weight and how you feel when traveling.

One way to make eating healthier when you travel is to avoid eating out as much as possible. Most hotels will rent a mini refrigerator to you for a few dollars a day or you can buy a cooler. Stocking some healthy foods like yogurt, cereal, milk, fruits, and even peanut butter and jelly will give you a break from the overly rich restaurant food. You can also do what one reporter who travels a lot suggested: Order a fruit basket to be delivered to your room on arrival. This gives you some healthy food that might include low-fat cheese, crackers, nuts, and cookies in addition to fruit. Even though this may not be as healthy as your diet at home, it will be much better than eating in a restaurant for every meal, and you'll save money as well.

In addition to thinking about food when you travel, it's also important to come prepared with the medications you might need in case of sudden illness. An internist who travels extensively herself has these suggestions for an emergency medical kit (Brand names are used only as examples. Any medication containing these ingredients would suffice.):

Emergency Medical Kit

Sudafed for nasal congestion (contains only pseudoephedrine)

Robitussin DM for coughs and congestion (contains only dextromethorphan and guaifenesin)

Antihistamines if you are prone to allergies

Imodium A-D for diarrhea

Ibuprofen for fever and body aches

Pepcid A-C or Tagamet for stomach acid

An over-the-counter sleep aid or sleeping pills (if you have used them before)

She cautions that you should never take any medication on a trip that you have not taken before. If you are going outside the United States, you might also want to get an antibiotic from your doctor to take for severe diarrhea caused by a bacterial infection.

Having all these medications with you can be a lifesaver on a trip. I experienced the need for these once when I was stricken with the worst upper respiratory infection of my life in France. Even though a physician friend was traveling with me, it was very difficult to get even the simplest over-the-counter cold medications because medications there are so different than in this country. I would have paid any price for Sudafed or Robitussin. Since that time, I don't leave home without them.

Another factor involved with travel is jet lag. The effects of jet lag are much the same as working overnights or shift schedules. They all involve a disruption of the natural Circadian rhythms of the body, our internal body clocks, which tell us when and how much to sleep.

Working Overnights

It is estimated that over one hundred million Americans have occasional sleep problems and one in six have chronic insomnia.[46] An occasional sleep problem might last a night or two and disappear, but for many broadcasters, poor sleep is the norm. In a survey done for the 1996 Radio-Television News Directors Association Conference, 51 percent of news directors surveyed reported that they had sleep problems.[47]

There are three types of sleep problems. You can suffer from *sleep onset insomnia* which means you can't get to sleep easily. *Sleep-maintenance insomnia* happens when you wake up and cannot go back to sleep or if you wake up intermittently for a total of more than thirty minutes per night. The final problem is *poor quality sleep* where you never reach a deep level of sleep.[48]

Extra adrenaline in the body can make good sleep difficult. Dr. Archibald Hart says, "Whenever adrenaline goes up, your sleep needs come down."[49] The adrenaline fools the body into thinking sleep is not necessary.

The amount of sleep that a person needs is very individual, but most studies say that seven hours is a minimum. Many of my clients tell me they routinely get only five or six hours of sleep because they're so energized by work. This may not seem too harmful, but lack of sleep has a cumulative effect on the body. Dr. Herbert Benson reports that most people can maintain performance with 60 percent to 70 percent of normal sleep, but irritability and fatigue will result.[50] Prolonged lack of sleep weakens our immune system making us more likely to get sick. Research is showing that even one bad night can reduce by as much as 30 percent the activity of natural infection-fighting immune cells in the body.[51]

Two conditions frequently encountered by broadcasters make good sleep difficult: jet lag and working overnight shifts.

Humans are unique in their abilities to disrupt their sleep. No other animal shifts sleep patterns as we do. Most animals who travel long distances, for example, move north and south.[52] They wouldn't think of traveling from the east coast to the west coast in one day changing four time zones.

It takes our bodies a full day to adjust to each time zone crossed. So if you're flying across the U.S., you will not feel your best until the third day you're there. Since many reporting assignments are only for a day, your body may never have a chance to adjust.

Working overnights or shifts that require you to work very late at night or begin early in the morning, also disrupts our body clocks. Despite this, in the U.S., around 10 percent of adults have jobs that require them to work odd hours. This takes a toll on the body. Your body needs a day for each hour your schedule is shifted to reset your body clock to your new schedule.[53] And if your schedule is not consistent as it would be with swing shifts, your body can't adapt.

Working overnights gives real meaning to the name "graveyard shift." There is actually a medical condition that you can develop with shift work called "shift maladaption syndrome." With this syndrome you may have chronic sleep problems, indigestion, ulcers, depression, chronic illnesses, and increased risk of miscarriage, heart attacks, and coronary artery disease.[54] Sleep disruption has a profoundly negative effect on the body.

Many people deal with overnight work by using coffee and sugar to keep going. When I work in newsrooms during a night shift, I notice that there's a coffee cup on almost everyone's desk. The problem with this is that because of your natural circadian rhythms "this is a time when your stomach has already closed down for the night."[55] It's not prepared to digest acidic liquids, and indigestion may follow. You may also tend to eat more because your appetite is confused. One television reporter told me that he's hungry all night when he's on overnights. His body can't figure out when to eat.

And when an overnight shift ends, the real challenge is getting to sleep and sleeping long enough. This same anchor said he sometimes comes home and naps throughout the day. Other people try to sleep all day. To accomplish this, they may turn to over-the-counter sleep aids which are actually antihistamines. These will cause a dry mouth and throat which makes on-air work difficult the next night. Plus, when you try to stop taking the sleep aids, it's even harder to get to sleep. This is true of prescription sleeping pills as well, which should be avoided except in emergency situations and used only with your doctor's recommendation.

Unfortunately, many broadcasters, like the general public, may also turn to alcohol to help them sleep. It is estimated that "20 percent of all insomniacs rely on alcohol to relax their muscles, ease their anxiety, and help them fall asleep."[56] The fact is, alcohol won't help you sleep, and it will contribute to poor sleep. The initial feeling is that alcohol relaxes you, but once your body has metabolized the alcohol, you are likely to awaken and not be able to go back to sleep. And when you do sleep, it will be poor. Just two alcoholic drinks at night effectively wipe out REM sleep which is when we dream and get our deepest sleep. [57]

So what can you do to aid sleep when your body clock is off? One dietary supplement that may work is melatonin. There have been no long term studies of melatonin, and it does not require government approval so it should not be used without consulting a physician. But many scientists are saying that melatonin is an effective, natural sleep aid.

They claim it "resets the body clock to match the bedside clock."[58]

There are many ways you can adjust your lifestyle to improve your sleep. First of all, avoid alcohol and caffeine before bedtime. Stop drinking alcohol two hours before bedtime and caffeine six hours before. Also be aware that nicotine disrupts sleep.

Increasing your exercise during the day will improve sleep, but stop your exercise at least three hours before you plan to sleep to let your body return to a relaxed state. You may also need to do aerobic exercise five times per week to improve sleep.

Use the relaxation techniques you read about in the last chapter to reduce stress before bedtime. Breathing exercises can be especially helpful (see Healthy Suggestions in Chapter 6). It's best not to get involved in phone calls or work stress for at least two hours before sleeping if you can help it. Going to sleep with too much on your mind may result in what one broadcaster described as "newsmares."

Keep your bedroom cool but increase the humidity. Also, avoid using your bed for activities like watching television or working. When you get in bed, you want your body to know that it's time to sleep. It helps to limit exposure to bright lights before sleeping as well. This will help your body know that it is time to begin producing melatonin.

Try to stay on the same sleep schedule if possible. Even if you have to get up at 2:00 a.m. and go to sleep at 6:00 p.m. for your particular schedule, you should stick to it even on weekends. You may want to go out and have fun late in the evenings on the weekends, but maintaining a consistent sleep schedule helps the body know when to sleep.

And finally, give yourself permission to sleep. It is a normal part of life. It's not wasted time, it's necessary time that allows you to be productive when you're awake. "My cheek has a love affair with my pillow," is what one Arabian client told me. That's a goal we can all strive for.

Healthy Suggestions

1 Prepare yourself for the next cold that catches you. Look through the medicines you now have and discard any that are multi-symptom. An advisory panel for the Food and Drug Administration suggests treating the symptoms of a cold individually. To do this use a single symptom medication. For nasal congestion look for a decongestant such as Sudafed that contains only pseudoephedrine. Look for a cough medication like Robitussin DM that contains only dextromethorphan and guaifenesin, a cough suppressant and expectorant. Make sure you have something to relieve aches and fever such as acetaminophen or ibuprofen. Avoid aspirin because it makes you more sensitive to vocal fold hemorrhage. And consider a non-medicinal saline nasal spray like Ocean or NaSal. Use these medications singly as your symptoms progress. It's also a good idea to check the expiration date on cold medications you might have on your medicine shelves. A medication that is old will not give you the relief you need.

2 Purchase a hygrometer and thermometer to monitor the humidity and temperature where you work and sleep. This is especially important if you feel the air in your newsroom is not comfortable or if you wake up with a dry throat. Since most of us spend the largest percentage of our days working and sleeping, these are two times when we want to be sure the air is within the comfort ranges of 73 to 79 degrees and 30 percent to 60 percent of humidity. You might want it even cooler when you're sleeping, but the humidity should remain within that range.

If you find you don't have enough humidity in your bedroom, consider using a warm-air ultrasonic humidifier. These can be purchased for around $100 and will add the needed humidity. The comfort range at work should be supplied as part of the building requirements. If you find it is not, talk to your supervisor about improving the air quality. Free-standing warm-air ultrasonic humidifiers can be added if the space is not too large, and high-efficiency particular arrestor air filters can help.

3 If you smoke, the single best thing you can do to improve your health and extend your life is to quit. The American Cancer Society offers a free "Quit Smoking Kit," and they have a quit smoking program called "FreshStart" that is designed to help you stop smoking in two weeks. To learn more about these programs call 800-ACS-2345. Programs are also available from the American Lung Association, the YMCA, and groups such as Smokers Anonymous and Smokenders. Most hospitals have programs as well. You can also combine the use of a nicotine patch with any of these groups to help you break the physiological addiction. It's easy to find help quitting. All you have to do is pick up the phone instead of your next cigarette.

4 Secondhand smoke is a health threat to all of us. Make a list of the places you frequent that allow smoking. If you stop for coffee or a drink several times a week in a place that allows smoking, consider going somewhere that's smoke free. And if you live with a smoker, make sure that person smokes in an area that will not allow the smoke to reach others. Remember the dangers of inhaling someone else's smoke.

5 Eye strain can be a problem when working on a computer. If you find you have headaches often, it may be from strain on your eyes. Ask your eye doctor to test your eyes for computer usage. You may need special glasses designed to adjust to the color and contrast of the letters on the computer screen. If you wear bifocals, it will be necessary to use different glasses for computer work so that you are not lifting your chin when looking at the monitor.

When you are working at the computer for long periods of time, look away often and focus your eyes on something about 20 feet away. Blink several times. This will give your eyes a break. Make certain that your monitor is 19 to 24 inches from your eyes and that it is directly in front of you. You should be looking slightly down at the monitor. An eye protection filter over your monitor will cut down on any glare.

6 One repetitive stress expert suggests you have somebody watch you at work on your computer. Have this person check your posture, head, arm, and wrist positions, and foot placement. When typing, your wrists should be in line with your forearms and hands. Your elbows should be bent at a 90 degree angle. Avoid up and down motions with the wrists while typing. Keyboard wrist supports can help, but be sure they are placed so that your elbows are always bent at a 90 degree angle and your wrists are in line with your forearms and hands. Keeping your keyboard low will help you maintain the 90 degree angle. Keep your feet flat on the floor or on a foot rest. Your chin should be parallel to the floor, and your shoulders should be relaxed. You should also vary your tasks. Don't type nonstop for long periods of

time. Recognize the need to stretch your body (see stretching exercises in Chapter 4).

7 If you're having trouble sleeping, keep a sleep diary where you record when you go to sleep and when you wake up. Also note how many times you awaken during each night. This will help you see what sleep patterns you have. It will also be of assistance if you go to your physician to discuss your sleep problem. If your doctor cannot help you with chronic insomnia problems, you might want to consult with a sleep disorder clinic. Write to either of these addresses to find an accredited sleep disorder center near you: National Sleep Foundation, 1367 Connecticut Ave., N.W., Suite 200, Washington, D.C. 20036; American Sleep Disorders Association, 1610 - 14th Street N.W., Suite 300, Rochester, MN 55901.

8 The audiotapes listed in the Helpful Resources section can be an aid in relaxing before going to sleep. A client of mine used one of these the week before she began a new television anchor job. She said it saved her life by allowing her to calm down enough from the anxiety she was experiencing to get a good night's sleep each night.

·8·

Helpful Resources

These telephone numbers and addresses will connect you with professionals or provide referrals to specialists in your area.

Anxiety, Stress, and Emotional Issues

American Psychiatric Association 202-682-6220
American Psychological Association 800-374-2721
American Psychological Association (public education info line) 800-964-2000
Anxiety Disorders Association of America 301-231-9350
Association for Applied Psychophysiology and Biofeedback 303-422-8436
National Association of Social Workers 202-408-8600
National Certification Board for Therapeutic Massage & Bodywork 800-296-0664
National Foundation for Depressive Illness 800-248-4344
National Mental Health Association 800-969-6642
Panic Disorder Education Program, Nat. Inst. Mental Health 800-64-panic

Environmental Health

Environmental Protection Agency Public Info Center
202-260-2080
Indoor Air Quality Information Clearinghouse
800-438-4318
National Institute of Environmental Health Sciences hot-line 800-643-4794

To find a consultant who specializes in environmental health, look for a professional who is a member of groups such as the American Institute of Architects, American Society of Mechanical Engineers, and the National Society of Professional Engineers.

Two companies in the Washington, D.C., area, who provide environmental consulting services are:

Feron Engineering Associates, David P. Feron, P.E. 301-948-8866
Greensweep, Mack B. Mahan, AIA, Vice President, 703-698-7202

Exercise

Aerobics & Fitness Association of America 800-445-5950
Aerobics & Fitness Foundation Association 800-446-2322
American College of Sports Medicine 317-637-9200
American Council on Exercise 800-825-3636
Cooper Institute for Aerobics Research 800-635-7050
The Fitness Connection 800-318-4024
National Academy of Sports Medicine 800-656-2739

Nutrition

American Dietetic Association 800-366-1655
Food and Nutrition Information Center, National Agri-
cultural Lib. 301-504-5719
International Bottled Water Association 800-water-11

Sleep

American Sleep Disorders Association
1610 - 14th Street NW, Suite 300
Rochester, MN 55901

National Sleep Foundation
1367 Connecticut Ave., N.W., Suite 200
Washington, D.C. 20036

Smoking

American Cancer Society 800-227-2345
American Lung Association 800-lung-usa
Cancer Information Service 800-422-6237

Helpful Resources: Audiotapes

There are many relaxation audiotapes available in bookstores and by mail. I have reviewed quite a few of them. The two tape series I found most helpful are from medical institutions that specialize in the treatment of stress. In addition to these, I have recorded two tapes available from Bonus Books that focus on relaxation for broadcasters. Also included here is the order information for meditation tapes by Stephen Levine.

• **The Mind/Body Medical Institute at Deaconess Hospital** offers more than a dozen tapes focusing on different techniques for relaxation. You can order tapes or request a list of all the tapes they offer by writing: The Mind/Body Medical Institute, Deaconess Hospital, Attn: Paul Baltos, One Deaconess Rd., Boston, MA 02215, 617-632-9525. Each tape is $10.

Two tapes that I have found especially helpful are:

(1) *Guided Visualization With Ocean Sounds/Breath and Body Awareness* (female voice)

Side 1 (24 minutes) is a guided body scan relaxation with guided visualization of a sandy ocean beach. Soothing ocean sounds in the background.

Side 2 (30 minutes) is a series of stretching exercises done in a sitting position to encourage a peaceful state of relaxation, awareness, and the elicitation of the relaxation response.

(2) *A Gift of Relaxation/Garden of Your Mind* (female voice)

Side 1 (20 minutes) focuses on guiding you through a body scan relaxation exercise with some simple deep breathing techniques. The tape ends with positive affirmations.

Side 2 (20 minutes) begins with body scan relaxation and breath awareness components and incorporates imagery of a lovely garden that you imagine. The tape ends with positive self statements and encouragement.

• **Mindfulness Meditation Practice Tapes with Jon Kabat-Zinn** Order from: Stress Reduction Tapes — P.O. Box 547, Lexington, MA 02173

Series I: Set of 2 tapes. The first tape includes a 45-minute guided body scan meditation and a 45-minute guided mindful hatha yoga session. The second tape includes a 45-minute guided sitting meditation and a 45-minute guided mindful hatha yoga session. Cost: $20 per set.

Series II: Set of 5 tapes. This set builds from 10-minute sessions to 30-minute sessions. Topics include guided sitting and lying meditations with focus on the awareness of breathing, a mountain meditation, a lake meditation, and silence with bells. Cost: $35 per set.

• **Meditation tapes by Stephen Levine** are available from Warm Rock Tapes, P.O. Box 108, Chamisal, NM 87521 or call 800-731-HEAL. His tapes are $9 and include topics such as grief, mindfulness, and the soft belly meditation.

• **Two tapes by Ann S. Utterback** focus on stress control and relaxation for broadcasters. Order these tapes from Bonus Books, 160 East Illinois Street, Chicago, IL 60611 or call 800-225-3775.

Coping With Stress for Broadcasters by Ann S. Utterback, Ph.D.

This tape has information about stress and how it affects broadcasters as well as a nine-minute guided relaxation period at the end of the tape.

Relaxation Practice by Ann S. Utterback, Ph.D.

This tape is designed to offer four different relaxation periods of ten minutes each. These include a progressive muscle relaxation exercise that can be done sitting at your desk, a guided visualization, a guided relaxation focusing on breathing, and ten minutes with the time noted for you at intervals so that you can relax in silence for any period of time up to ten minutes. Either side of the tape can be done as a longer relaxation period of 20 minutes by combining the two areas.

·9·

Suggested Reading

American Cancer Society, "Cancer: Basic Facts," Cancer Facts & Figures."

Anderson, Bob. *Stretching for Everyday Fitness and for Running, Tennis, Racquetball, Cycling, Swimming, Golf, and other Sports.* Bolinas, CA: Shelter Publications, 1980.

Bailey, Covert. *The New Fit or Fat.* Boston: Houghton Mifflin Co., 1991.

_____. *Smart Exercise.* Boston: Houghton Mifflin Co., 1994.

Benson, Herbert. *The Relaxation Response.* New York: Avon, 1975.

Benson, Herbert, and Stuart, Eileen M. *The Wellness Book: The Comprehensive Guide to Maintaining Health and Treating Stress-Related Illness.* New York: Simon & Schuster, 1992.

Borysenko, Joan. *Minding the Body, Mending the Mind.* New York: Bantam Books, 1987.

Brody, Jane. *Jane Brody's Cold & Flu Fighter.* New York: W.W. Norton & Co., 1995.

_____. *Jane Brody's Nutrition Book.* New York: W.W. Norton & Co., 1981.

Brumet, Robert. *Finding Yourself in Transition: Using Life's Changes for Spiritual Awakening.* Unity Village, Mo.: Unity Books, 1995.

Butterworth, Eric. *Spiritual Economics: Reshaping Your Attitudes About Money, Spirituality, and Personal Prosperity.* Unity Village, Mo.: Unity Books, 1983.

Dacher, Elliott. *PNI: Psychoneuroimmunology The New Mind/ Body Healing Program.* New York: Paragon House, 1991.

Davis, Martha; Eshelman, Elizabeth Robbins; and McKay, Matthew. *The Relaxation & Stress Reduction Workbook.* Oakland, CA.: New Harbinger Publications, Inc., 1995.

Domar, Alice D., and Dreher, Henry. *Healing Mind, Healthy Woman: Using the Mind-Body Connection to Manage Stress and Take Control of Your Life.* New York: Henry Holt and Co., 1996.

Eliot, Robert S., and Breo, Dennis. *Is It Worth Dying For?* New York: Bantam Books, 1984.

Frankl, Viktor E. *Man's Search for Meaning.* New York: Simon & Schuster Inc., 1959.

Friedman, Meyer, and Ulmer, Diane. *Treating Type A Behavior and Your Heart.* New York: Fawcett Crest, 1984.

Hanh, Thich Nhat. *Peace is Every Step: The Path of Mindfulness in Everyday Life.* New York: Bantam Books, 1991.

Hartmand, Cherry, and Huffaker, Julie Sheldon. *The Fearless Flyer: How to Fly in Comfort and Without Trepidation.* Portland, Oregon: Eighth Mountain Press, 1995.

Hart, Archibald D. *The Hidden Link Between Adrenalin and Stress.* Dallas: Word Publishing, 1991.

Human Nutrition Information Service. "The Food Guide Pyramid." Washington, D.C.: United States Department of Agriculture, 1992.

Inlander, Charles B., and Moran, Cynthia K. *77 Ways to Beat Colds and Flu.* New York: Walker & Co., 1994.

Ivker, Robert S. *Sinus Survival.* New York: G. P. Putnam's Sons, 1995.

Jafolla, Richard and Mary-Alice. *Nourishing the Life Force.* Unity Village, Mo.: Unity Books, 1984.

Kabat-Zinn, Jon. *Full Catastrophe Living: Using the Wisdom of Your Body and Mind to Face Stress, Pain, and Illness.* New York: Dell Publishing, 1990.

_____. *Wherever You Go There You Are: Mindfulness Meditation in Everyday Life.* New York: Hyperion, 1994.

Kirsta, Alix. *The Book of Stress Survival: Identifying and Reducing the Stress in Your Life.* New York: Simon & Schuster, 1986.

Levine, Stephen. *A Gradual Awakening.* Garden City, N.Y.: Anchor Press, 1979.

_____. *A Year to Live.* New York: Bell Tower, 1997.

_____. *Guided Meditations, Explorations and Healings.* New York: Anchor Books, 1991.

Lidell, Lucy. *The Sivananda Companion to Yoga.* New York: Simon & Schuster, 1983.

Mason, L. John. *Guide to Stress Reduction.* Berkeley, Ca.: Celestial Arts, 1980.

Northrup, Christiane. *Women's Bodies, Women's Wisdom.* New York: Bantam Books, 1994.

Ornish, Dean. *Dr. Dean Ornish's Program for Reversing Heart Disease.* New York: Ballantine Books, 1990.

Reiter, Russel J., and Robinson, Jo. *Melatonin: Your Body's Natural Wonder Drug.* New York: Bantam Books, 1995.

Sears, Barry, and Lawren, Bill. *The Zone: A Dietary Road Map.* New York: Harper Collins, 1995.

Sehnert, Keith W. *Stress/Unstress.* Minneapolis: Augsburg Publishing, 1981.

St. James, Elaine. *Inner Simplicity: 100 Ways to Regain Peace and Nourish Your Soul.* New York: Hyperion, 1995.

Summers, Caryn, ed. *Inspirations for Caregivers.* Mt. Shasta, Ca.: Commune-a-Key Publishing, 1993.

Utterback, Ann S. *Broadcast Voice Handbook: How to Polish Your On-Air Delivery.* Chicago: Bonus Books, 1995.

Walz, Judy Ann. *Quick Fixes to Change Your Life: Making Healthy Choices.* Midland, Ga.: Creative Health Services, Inc., 1995.

Wilson, Paul. *Instant Calm: Over 100 Easy-to-Use Techniques for Relaxing Mind and Body.* New York: Penguin Books, 1995.

Notes

Chapter 1

1 *In The Heart Lies The Deathless,* Audio tape, Stephen Levine, Sounds True Recordings, 1989 (2, 90-minute tapes).

2 Stephen Levine, *A Gradual Awakening* (Garden City, N.Y.: Anchor Press, 1979) 6.

Chapter 2

1 "Heart of Destruction," song by Ferron, Nemesis Publishing, 1990.

2 Joan Borysenko, Ph.D., *Minding The Body, Mending The Mind* (New York: Bantam Books, 1987) 15.

3 Herbert Benson, M.D., Eileen M. Stuart, R.N., *The Wellness Book* (New York: Simon and Schuster, 1992) 9.

4 Ibid., 12.

5 Robert S. Eliot, M.D., Dennis L. Breo, *Is It Worth Dying For?* (New York: Bantam Books, 1984) 160.

Chapter 3

1 Robert S. Eliot, M.D. and Dennis L. Breo, *Is It Worth Dying For?* (New York: Bantam Books, 1984) 15.

2 Dr. Howard Seiden, "Karoshi Killing Thousands in Japan," *Montreal Gazette* 2/4/95, Final Edition, sec. Living; Your Health: J6.

3 Dr. Archibald D. Hart, *The Hidden Link Between Adrenalin and Stress* (Dallas: Word Publishing, 1991) 14.

4 Ibid., 49.

5 Jim Cairo, "Reflections on a View From Outer Space," *Unity Magazine,* 10/94, 62.

6 Dr. Archibald D. Hart, *The Hidden Link Between Adrenalin and Stress* (Dallas: Word Publishing, 1991) viii.

7 Robert S. Eliot, M.D., Dennis L. Breo, *Is It Worth Dying For?* (New York: Bantam Books, 1984) 23.

8 Alix Kirsta, *The Book of Stress Survival* (New York: Simon and Schuster, Inc., 1986) 6.

9 Dr. Archibald D. Hart, *The Hidden Link Between Adrenalin and Stress* (Dallas: Word Publishing, 1991) 15.

10 Ibid., 17.

11 Ibid., 55.

12 Covert Bailey, *The New Fit or Fat* (Boston: Houghton Mifflin Company, 1991) 97.

13 "Better Tomorrow: Can Stress Reduction Hasten Healing?," *Prevention* 5/96: 63.

14 Covert Bailey, *The New Fit or Fat* (Boston: Houghton Mifflin Company, 1991) 271.

15 Meyer Friedman, M.D., and Diane Ulmer, R.N., M.S., *Treating Type A Behavior and Your Heart* (New York: Fawcett Crest, 1984) 33.

16 Dr. Archibald D. Hart, *The Hidden Link Between Adrenalin and Stress* (Dallas: Word Publishing, 1991) 162.

17 Keith W. Sehnert, M.D., *Stress/Unstress* (Minneapolis: Augsburg Publishing, 1981) 43–44.

18 "Panic Disorder" (Pamphlet), *U.S. Department of Health and Human Services* 1991.

19 Anxiety Disorders Association of America.

20 Thomas H. Holmes and Richard R. Rahe, "Holmes-Rahe Stress Test." Reprinted with permission from *Journal of Psychosomatic Research* 11(2), 1967: 213–218, Elsevier Science Inc.

21 Herbert Benson, M.D., *The Relaxation Response* (New York: Avon, 1975) 56.

22 Caryn Summers, R.N., Editor, *Inspirations for Caregivers* (Mount Shasta, California: Commune-a-Key Publishing, 1993) 203.

Chapter 4

1 Dean Ornish, M.D., *Dr. Dean Ornish's Program for Reversing Heart Disease* (New York: Ballantine Books, 1990) 324.

2 Russell R. Pate, Ph.D., et.al., "Physical Activity and Public Health," *JAMA* Vol 273, No. 5 (2/1/95): 403.

3 Covert Bailey, *Smart Exercise* (Boston: Houghton Mifflin, 1994) 6–7.

4 Dean Ornish, M.D., *Dr. Dean Ornish's Program for Reversing Heart Disease* (New York: Ballantine Books, 1990) 325.

5 Russell R. Pate, Ph.D., et.al., "Physical Activity and Public Health," *JAMA* Vol 273, No. 5 (2/1/95): 404.

6 Covert Bailey, *Smart Exercise* (Boston: Houghton Mifflin, 1994) 273.

7 Steven N. Blair, PED, et.al., "Changes in Physical Fitness and All-Cause Mortality: A Perspective Study of Healthy and Unhealthy Men," *JAMA* Vol 273, No. 14 (4/12/95): 1097.

8 "Exercise," *Nutrition Action Healthletter* 12/95: 5.

9 Constance Cardozo, "What 'Fit' Means Now," *Working Woman* 4/92: 85.

10 Dean Ornish, M.D., *Dr. Dean Ornish's Program for Reversing Heart Disease* (New York: Ballantine Books, 1990) 2.

11 Russell R. Pate, Ph.D., et.al., "Physical Activity and Public Health," *JAMA* Vol 273, No. 5 (2/1/95): 404.

12 Dean Ornish, M.D., *Dr. Dean Ornish's Program for Reversing Heart Disease* (New York : Ballantine Books, 1990) 330–331.

Chapter 5

1 Francine Hermelin, "The Food-Stress Link," *Working Woman* 5/93: 92.

2 Richard and Mary-Alice Jafolla, *Nourishing the Life Force* (Unity Village, Missouri: Unity Books, 1985) 9.

3 Barry Sears, Ph.D. and Bill Lawren, *The Zone: A Dietary Road Map* (New York: Harper Collins, 1995) 77.

4 Christiane Northrup, M.D., *Women's Bodies, Women's Wisdom* (New York : Bantam Books, 1994) 566.

5 "Living Well," *Living Fit* 5-6/96: 26.

6 "Body and Mind," *Prevention* 11/95: 80.

7 Herbert Benson, M.D. and Eileen M. Stuart, R.N., *The Wellness Book* (New York: Simon and Schuster, 1992) 133.

8 Kotsonis and Mackey, eds., chapter by Steven N. Blair P.Ed., *Nutrition in the 90s* (New York: Marcel Dekker, 1994) 67.

9 Judy Walz, R.N., *Quick Fixes to Change Your Life* (Midland, Georgia: Creative Health Services, Inc., 1995) 60.

10 "The Mini-Meals Are Coming," *Prevention* 5/95: 82.

11 Jane E. Brody, *Jane Brody's Nutrition Book* (New York: W.W. Norton & Company, 1981) 35.

12 Susan M. Kleiner and Maggie Greenwood-Robinson, "Feeding Your Pace," *Shape* 5/96: 146.

13 Jane E. Brody, *Jane Brody's Nutrition Book* (New York: W.W. Norton & Company, 1981) 49.

14 *The New Carbohydrate Gram Counter* (New York: Dell Publishing Company, 1965).

15 Human Nutrition Information Service, *The Food Guide Pyramid* (Washington, D.C.: United States Department of Agriculture, 1992) 13.

16 "Sweets to Die For," *Nutrition Action Healthletter* 6/96: 5.

17 Human Nutrition Information Service, *The Food Guide Pyramid* (Washington, D.C.: United States Department of Agriculture, 1992) 25–27.

18 Christiane Northrup, M.D., *Women's Bodies, Women's Wisdom* (New York: Bantam Books, 1994) 586.

19 Jane E. Brody, *Jane Brody's Nutrition Book* (New York: W.W. Norton & Company, 1981) 235.

20 Robert S. Ivker, *Sinus Survival* (New York: G. P. Putnam's Sons, 1995) 132.

21 "The Latest Caffeine Scorecard," *FDA Consumer* 3/84.

22 Jane E. Brody, *Jane Brody's Nutrition Book* (New York: W.W. Norton & Co., 1981) 235.

23 Ibid., 239.

24 Dean Ornish, M.D., *Dr. Dean Ornish's Program for Reversing Heart Disease* (New York: Ballantine Books, 1990) 272.

25 Jane E. Brody, *Jane Brody's Nutrition Book* (New York: W.W. Norton & Co., 1981) 243.

26 Ibid., 128.

27 Covert Bailey, *The New Fit or Fat* (Boston: Houghton Mifflin Company, 1991) 117.

28 Dean Ornish, *Dr. Dean Ornish's Program for Reversing Heart Disease* (New York: Ballantine Books, 1990) 275.

29 Human Nutrition Information Services, *The Food Guide Pyramid* (Washington, D.C.: United States Department of Agriculture, 1992) 16.

30 Jane E. Brody, *Jane Brody's Nutrition Book* (New York: W.W. Norton & Company, 1981) 261.

31 Dean Ornish, M.D., *Dr. Dean Ornish's Program for Reversing Heart Disease* (New York : Ballantine Books, 1990) 278.

32 Human Nutrition Information Service, *The Food Guide Pyramid* (Washington, D.C.: United States Department of Agriculture, 1992) 17.

33 Human Nutrition Information Service, *The Food Guide Pyramid* (Washington, D.C.: United States Department of Agriculture, 1992) 17.

34 Elizabeth Austin, "Water Bearers," *Shape* 7/95: 74.

35 Robert S. Ivker, *Sinus Survival* (New York: G. P. Putnam's Sons, 1995) 138–9.

36 Jane E. Brody, *Jane Brody's Nutrition Book* (New York: W.W. Norton & Company, 1981) 219.

37 "Water: When Eight Cups Is Not Enough," *Shape* 3/95: 24.

38 Covert Bailey, *Smart Exercise* (Boston: Houghton Mifflin Company, 1994) 215.

39 Elizabeth Austin, "Waters Bearers," *Shape* 7/95: 79.

40 Marty Munson with Carol Spiciarich, "Don't Let Your Body Run Dry," *Prevention* 7/96: 90.

41 Robert S. Ivker, *Sinus Survival* (New York: G.P. Putnam's Sons, 1995) 139.

42 Covert Bailey, *Smart Exercise* (New York: Ballantine Books, 1994) 222–23.

43 Ibid., 217.

44 Leroy R. Perry, Jr., "Are You Drinking Enough Water?," *Parade* 10/22/89: 5.

45 Jane E. Brody, *Jane Brody's Nutrition Book* (New York : W.W. Norton & Company, 1981) 221.

46 Marty Munson with Carol Spiciarich, "Don't Let Your Body Run Dry," *Prevention* 7/96: 91.

47 Christiane Northrup, M.D., *Women's Bodies, Women's Wisdom* (New York: Bantam Books, 1994) 575.

48 Covert Bailey, *Smart Exercise* (Boston: Houghton Mifflin Company, 1994) 217.

Chapter 6

1 Richard Eberhart, *Collected Poems, 1930-1960* (New York: Oxford University Press, 1960).

2 Jon Kabat-Zinn, Ph.D., *Full Catastrophe Living: Using the Wisdom of Your Body and Mind to Face Stress, Pain, and Illness* (New York: Dell Publishing, 1990) 20.

3 Jean Callahan, "Relax," *Self* 6/95: 130.

4 Alice D. Domar, Ph.D. and Henry Dreher, *Healing Mind, Healthy Woman* (New York: Henry Holt and Company, 1996) 41.

5 "Relax Into Better Health," *Prevention* 5/94: 16.

6 Bernadette P. Swanson, "Healing Sounds," *Unity Magazine* 10/96: p. 47. Note: Calm brain waves are 7.8 cycles per second and the vibration of the earth is the Schumann resonance=8 cycles per second.

7 Herbert Benson, M.D., Eileen M. Stuart, *The Wellness Book: The Comprehensive Guide to Maintaining Health and Treating Stress-Related Illness* (New York: Simon & Schuster, 1992) 35.

8 Alix Kirsta, *The Book of Stress Survival: Identifying and Reducing the Stress in Your Life* (New York: Simon & Schuster, 1986) 101.

9 *The Art of Mindful Living,* audio tape, Thich Nhat Hanh, Sounds True Recording, 1991 (180 min.).

10 Jon Kabat-Zinn, *Wherever You Go There You Are: Mindfulness Meditation in Everyday Life* (New York: Hyperion, 1994) 96–7.

11 Ibid., 5.

12 Dean Ornish, M.D., *Dr. Dean Ornish's Program for Reversing Heart Disease* (New York: Ballantine Books, Inc., 1990) 172.

13 Barbara Harris, "Mind Matters: You Are What You Think," *Shape* 8/96: 14.

14 Dean Ornish, M.D., *Dr. Dean Ornish's Program for Reversing Heart Disease* (New York: Ballantine Books, Inc., 1990) 175.

15 Ibid., 174.

16 Eric Butterworth, *Spiritual Economics: Reshaping Your Attitudes About Money, Spirituality, and Personal Prosperity* (Unity Village, MO: Unity Books, 1983) 55.

17 Ibid., 42.

18 Alice D. Domar, Ph.D. and Henry Dreher, *Healing Mind, Healthy Woman: Using the Mind-Body Connection to Manage Stress and Take Control of Your Life* (New York: Henry Holt and Company, 1996) 116.

19 Herbert Benson, M.D., Eileen M. Stuart, *The Wellness Book: The Comprehensive Guide to Maintaining Health and Treating Stress-Related Illness* (New York: Simon & Schuster Inc., 1992) 235.

20 Viktor E. Frankl, *Man's Search for Meaning* (New York: Simon & Schuster Inc., 1959) 74.

21 Paul Wilson, *Instant Calm: Over 100 Easy-to-Use Techniques for Relaxing Mind and Body* (New York: Penguin Books, 1995) 89.

22 John Milton, *"Paradise Lost,"* Lines 254–5.

23 Richard Kehl, *Silver Departures* (La Jolla, CA: A Star & Elephant Book, 1983) 53.

24 Alice D. Domar, Ph.D. and Henry Dreher, *Healing Mind, Healthy Woman: Using the Mind-Body Connection to manage Stress and Take Control of Your Life* (New York: Henry Holt and Company, Inc., 1996) 117.

25 Christy Cave (Host), *The Reporters,* Flagship Station, University of Maryland, College Park, MD.

26 Dean Ornish, M.D., *Dr. Dean Ornish's Program for Reversing Heart Disease* (New York : Ballantine Books, 1990) 143.

27 *Creating Health,* Audiotape, Chris Northrup, M.D., Sounds True Audio, 1993 (180 min.).

28 L. John Mason, Ph.D., *Guide To Stress Reduction* (Berkeley, CA: Celestial Arts, 1980) 33.

29 Stephen Levine, *A Gradual Awakening* (Garden City, NY: Anchor Books, 1979) 115.

30 "Think Yourself Healthy," *Prevention* 8/96: 146.

Chapter 7

1 Caryn Summers, R.N., *Inspirations for Caregivers* (Mount Shasta, CA: Commune-A-Key Publishing, 1993) 239.

2 Charles B. Inlander and Cynthia K. Moran, *77 Ways to Beat Colds and Flu* (New York: Walker and Company, 1994) 7.

3 Jane Brody, *Jane Brody's Cold & Flu Fighter* (New York: W.W. Norton & Company, 1995) 9.

4 Ibid., 44.

5 Charles B. Inlander and Cynthia K. Moran, *77 Ways to Beat Colds and Flu* (New York: Walker and Company, 1994) 45.

6 Jane Brody, *Jane Brody's Cold & Flu Fighter* (New York: W.W. Norton & Company, 1995) 23.

7 Charles B. Inlander and Cynthia K. Moran, *77 Ways to Beat Colds and Flu* (New York: Walker and Company, 1994) 31.

8 Jane Brody, *Jane Brody's Cold & Flu Fighter* (New York: W.W. Norton & Company, 1995) 22.

9 Sharon Stocker, "How Not to Get Sick," *Prevention* 12/96: pp. 86–7.

10 Charles B. Inlander and Cynthia K. Moran, *77 Ways to Beat Colds and Flu* (New York: Walker and Company, 1994) 56.

11 Stephanie Newman, "When Your Office Makes You Sick," *Lear's* January, 1993: 30.

12 Jonathan E. Fielding, M.D., M.P.H. and Kenneth J. Phenow, M.S., M.P.H., "Health Effects of Involuntary Smoking," *American Cancer Society* 1989: 1.

13 American Cancer Society, "Tobacco Use," *Cancer Facts & Figures — 1996,* 24.

14 Joel Achenbach, "Going Up In Smoke," *The Washington Post* 7/29/94, Final ed., sec. D: 5.

15 Dean Ornish, M.D., *Dr. Dean Ornish's Program for Reversing Heart Disease* (New York : Ballantine Books, 1990) 274.

16 Ibid., 305.

17 American Cancer Society, "Tobacco Use," *Cancer Facts & Figures — 1996,* 25.

18 Dean Ornish, M.D., *Dr. Dean Ornish's Program for Reversing Heart Disease* (New York : Ballantine Books, 1990) 306.

19 Ibid., 307.

20 Robert S. Eliot, M.D. and Dennis L. Breo, *Is It Worth Dying For?* (New York: Bantam Books, 1984) 196.

21 American Cancer Society, "Tobacco Use," *Cancer Facts & Figures — 1996,* 24.

22 American Cancer Society, "Selected Cancers," *Cancer Facts & Figures — 1996,* 10.

23 American Cancer Society, "Cancer: Basic Facts," *Cancer Facts & Figures — 1996,* 1.

24 American Cancer Society, "Tobacco Use," *Cancer Facts & Figures — 1996,* 24.

25 Dean Ornish, M.D., *Dr. Dean Ornish's Program for Reversing Heart Disease* (New York: Ballantine Books, 1990) 65.

26 American Cancer Society, *The Decision Is Yours,* 1977 ed.: 1.

27 Jonathan E. Fielding, M.D., M.P.H. and Kenneth J. Phenow, M.S., M.P.H., "Health Effects of Involuntary Smoking," *American Cancer Society* 1989: 2.

28 American Cancer Society, "Prevention," *Cancer Facts & Figures— 1995,* 21.

29 American Cancer Society, "What Should You Know?," *The Smoke Around Us,* 1995: 1.

30 "Self-Care," *Prevention* 3/94: 75.

31 "In Shape: Puff the Tragic Dragon," *Shape* 6/96: 28.

32 American Cancer Society, "When Smokers Quit," 1996: 3.

33 Sarah Glazer, "A Modern Malady," *The Washington Post* 3/12/96, Final ed., sec. Health: 13.

34 Ibid.

35 Ibid., 15.

36 Steve Schwade with Teri Walsh, "Read This Before You Fly," *Prevention* 6/96: 103.

37 Cherry Hartman and June Sheldon Huffaker, *The Fearless Flyer* (Portland: The Eighth Mountain Press, 1995) 110.

38 Ibid., 103.

39 Jerrold Nadler, Member of Congress, "Every Time You Fly, You Could Get Sick," *Letter to Members of Congress of the United States* 4/11/96.

40 Cherry Hartman and Julie Sheldon Huffaker, *The Fearless Flyer* (Portland: The Eighth Mountain Press, 1996) 110.

41 Ibid., 111.

42 "What Pulls The Plug," *Prevention* 7/96: 89.

43 Cherry Hartman and Julie Sheldon Huffaker, *The Fearless Flyer* (Portland: The Eighth Mountain Press, 1996) 89.

44 "Wish Upon A Starbucks," *Nutrition Action Healthletter* 12/96: 4, and "Sweets To Die For," *Nutrition Action Healthletter* 6/96: 5.

45 "Hard Artery Cafe," *Nutrition Action Healthletter* 10/96: 5.

46 Herbert Benson, M.D., Eileen M. Stuart, *The Wellness Book* (New York: Simon & Schuster, 1992) 289.

47 Survey done by Sidney Bundy and the RTNDA for Radio Round-table entitled, "Managing Stress Before It Manages You," 10/96.

48 Herbert Benson, M.D. and Eileen M. Stuart, *The Wellness Book* (New York: Simon & Schuster, 1992) 290.

49 Dr. Archibald D. Hart, *The Hidden Link Between Adrenalin and Stress* (Dallas: Word Publishing, 1991) 131.

50 Herbert Benson, M.D. and Eileen M. Stuart, *The Wellness Book* (New York: Simon & Schuster, 1992) 292–3.

51 Dawn Welch, "Sick and Tired," *Shape* 6/95: 22.

52 Russel J. Reiter, Ph.D., and Jo Robinson, *Melatonin* (New York: Bantam Books, 1995) 110.

53 Ibid., 113.

54 Ibid.

55 Ibid.

56 Russel J. Reiter, Ph.D., and Jo Robinson, *Melatonin* (New York: Bantam Books, 1995) 95.

57 Christiane Northrup, *Women's Bodies, Women's Wisdom* (New York: Bantam Books, 1994) 615.

58 Russel J. Reiter, Ph.D., and Jo Robinson, *Melatonin* (New York: Bantam Books, 1995) 4.

Index

Also Available: